FLEA MARKET
secrets

FLEA MARKET
secrets

AN INDISPENSABLE GUIDE TO WHERE TO GO AND WHAT TO BUY

GERALDINE JAMES

CICO BOOKS

LONDON NEW YORK

Published in 2015 by CICO Books
An imprint of Ryland Peters & Small Ltd

20–21 Jockey's Fields   341 E 116th St
London WC1R 4BW   New York, NY 10029

www.rylandpeters.com

10 9 8 7 6 5 4 3 2 1

A CIP catalog record for this book is available from the
Library of Congress and the British Library.

ISBN: 978 1 78249 186 6

Printed in China

Editor: Helen Ridge
Designer: Geoff Borin
Photographer: Andrew Wood

Managing editor: Gillian Haslam
In-house designer: Fahema Khanam
Art director: Sally Powell
Production manager: Gordana Simakovic
Publishing manager: Penny Craig
Publisher: Cindy Richards

CONTENTS

INTRODUCTION

HUNTING FOR TREASURES HIDDEN AMONGST THE TRASH AT FLEA
MARKETS IS A TRULY ADDICTIVE PASTIME. ONCE YOU'VE BEEN
BITTEN BY THE BUG, YOU WILL SOON FIND YOURSELF LOOKING OUT
FOR FLEA MARKETS WHEREVER YOU HAPPEN TO BE IN THE WORLD!

When I first became a retail buyer for homeware and gifts after a number of years as a fashion buyer, I knew it was a way for me to indulge in something completely new and unique. I started going to trade shows and reading interior design magazines, which I loved. I discovered antique markets and vintage fairs, and found them so utterly thrilling that I became obsessed. I developed a real hunger to find the most exciting things I could, not only for my work but also for my home. Along the way, I have found some truly astonishing items, from mirrors, cabinets, and vases to garden benches, pots, and statues—the list is endless—and the search is far from over.

I refer to my current role as a "jobby" (hobby/job) because the two things have become so intertwined, and I find any excuse to go to the

ABOVE A perfect example of the eclectic assortment of treasures for sale at a flea market —a pair of vintage paintings of children, an amusing sign, and an animal skull, complete with horns.

RIGHT Treasure hunting at the Round Top market in Texas. A clear blue sky and endless miles of vendors makes it both exciting and a little daunting for the first-time visitor.

OPPOSITE One of the wooden houses in Round Top, selling all manner of vintage accessories. Rummaging and finding just the right thing is part of the thrill of antiquing.

ABOVE Big Daddy's is a huge treasure trove in San Francisco. It's full of wonderful surprises, and this display is no exception. Stacked up on this shelving unit are piles of old ledgers, now slightly battered and worn. It's now hard to believe there was a time when all business transactions were recorded by hand!

RIGHT A study in monochrome. Many vendors display items with real skill and an eye for the aesthetic. An industrial fan from the 1940s takes center stage (always have the wiring checked before using old electrical equipment), supported by a vintage alarm clock which has seen better days and two detailed black-and-white prints.

markets. My advice to those just starting their own flea-market hunting is to be patient—you will never find what you are looking for on your first trip. However, if you are prepared to work at it, you will discover all sorts of treasures, but be aware also that you will end up buying things you didn't know you wanted. I cherish the pieces I've found, enjoying their history and appreciating their rarity. They all add something special to my home. For me, it's all about their individual charm and decorative value, and knowing that no one else will have them.

For this book, I have traveled as far afield as the markets of the south of France, and to California and Texas, where I experienced the renowned Round Top Antiques Market, which I loved. Staying at my friend Rachel Ashwell's guesthouse, The Prairie, was truly special, and Rachel, the creator of the Shabby Chic Couture brand and a real veteran of treasure hunting, has generously taught me all about patina, mixing vintage with new, and so much more.

I love how a new industry has emerged from the marketing of vintage objects, with young entrepreneurs realizing that using or making things

BELOW A stall of mixed ephemera at Shepton Mallet antique market, in the south of England. The main theme here is transport, with paintings of boats and racing cars, a model ship and a toy truck. However, as with many stalls, other assorted items have crept in too, such as the antique clock, the vintage road sign, and the pub sign depicting Robin Hood.

from existing vintage finds, or simply restoring them or giving something a new purpose, is the ultimate in recycling. I like to think that the vintage trend is responsible for unwanted items being given a new lease of life. Many such items were made by skilled craftsmen and artisans from the past, and it's good to keep their creations alive in a modern home.

I have discovered a lifelong passion and now, wherever I travel in the world, the first thing I do is look up where and when the antique markets and vintage fairs are held and head to them. This is a fabulous way of learning about local culture and how people live their lives, the style of their furniture, the way that they cook, and so on. In pursuit of this passion, I have influenced many friends, who have how become as obsessed as I am, and I have enjoyed watching their collections grow. I also get a kick out of lending my own flea-market china collection to friends. It's good to share and let others enjoy your passion.

Good luck and happy hunting!

LEFT This is a typical stall at Round Top market in Texas. I find it easy to engage with the vendor when there is such a mixture of items—the stories behind the items flow, and this is one of the things that make treasure hunting such fun. The huge ice cream sign dates back to the 1940s and the Florida-based DeConna company. The plaster clown's head probably came from a circus.

BELOW Another eclectic Round Top stall. Here the everyday goods for sale have probably come from a house clearance.

my golden rules

TO GET THE MOST OUT OF YOUR FLEA MARKET ADVENTURES, IT DOES PAY TO PLAN AHEAD. THESE ARE MY TEN GOLDEN RULES, BASED ON VISITING HUNDREDS OF MARKETS OVER THE YEARS.

1 COMFORT

Check the weather forecast and make sure you are geared up for whatever the weather throws at you—for HEAT, a hat and suntan cream; for RAIN, a hooded raincoat (you won't be able to carry an umbrella); for COLD, plenty of layers (feet and hands get the coldest). Wear comfortable flat shoes, and a cross-body bag so your hands are free.

2 BE PREPARED

Always withdraw cash from the bank before the trip—you will get a better bargain and it aids your negotiations. Set your limit of spending. If you are looking for something specific, take room measurements as dimensions are vital. Take a notebook and pen, plus a torch if it's early morning.

3 PLOT YOUR DAY

Download the map of the market you are going to. Set your priorities—remember the early bird catches the worm, so take a fast overview of the whole market when you arrive and then go back slowly around the stalls (you don't always spot what you are looking for first time; you have to be patient and be prepared to keep at it).

4 RESEARCH

I find it quite important to do some research beforehand, particularly if you are looking for something specific. If the provenance is important to you, get some idea of the sort of price you will be expected to pay, pay attention to what authentic markings are, take a picture on your phone of any reference. It all helps if you know what you are talking about.

5 TRANSPORT

How will you get your purchases home? Take into account the cost of transport if you are buying something big. Bear this in mind when making a purchase as it may actually make what you thought was a bargain something a bit costly. Most big markets will have companies on the ground who will be happy to deliver your purchases, so get estimates of the costings.

6 INTERIOR SCHEMES

Usually the vintage items are the final dressing for a room. They are what adds the charm and character. I always find that if I have an overall vision of what I am trying to achieve, it helps with my selection. Having said that, some of my favorite possessions have been very unexpected buys, but nevertheless I also have things that I snapped up on impulse and now regret buying!

7 COLLECTING

Collecting is fun, and I have many varied collections. They are a really good way of being focused and when you have all your things on display together at home, it looks well thought out and considered. Collections of white jugs and pitchers, portraits, oil on canvas, floral china, mismatched cups and saucers, colored glassware—the list is endless. It makes your flea-market foraging more focused.

8 LOOK BEYOND THE AGE

By this I mean, look at what can be achieved by cleaning, fixing, restoring. Something that looks quite dirty or damaged can be restored quite simply with little cost. Some things are simply beyond repair, but if you have the time and inclination to fix something or if an expert is needed, check what this will mean. In these days of modern technology, you can research while out and about.

9 INFORMATION

Ask the vendor for as much history of the item as possible as it is satisfying to have the story, where it's from, age, and so on. It's all part of the charm and it's these things that create not necessarily the value of a piece but the interest .

10 DON'T BE AFRAID

Finally, use your gut instinct! If you love it and the price is right, BUY IT! In the end, this is what really matters. Do you want to live with it? If so, don't hang about. I can't tell you how many times I've dithered and come back to get an item and found it has gone. The disappointment is huge.

CHAPTER 1:
FURNITURE

SEATING

THE SEARCH FOR CHAIRS CAN BE A CHALLENGE BECAUSE YOU USUALLY
NEED MORE THAN ONE, OFTEN A PAIR, AND SOMETIMES EVEN A MATCHING SET.
WHETHER YOU'RE AFTER A CLUB CHAIR IN WORN LEATHER, A SET OF OLD SCHOOL
CHAIRS FOR THE DINING TABLE, OR MAYBE SOMETHING A LITTLE MORE DELICATE,
BE PREPARED TO HUNT FOR SEVERAL MONTHS TO GET EXACTLY WHAT YOU WANT.

SOFAS AND ARMCHAIRS

Unless you are flea-market-shopping with the aim purely of reselling, the most important factor to bear in mind is that you must buy what you like and know that you can live with it. It must also do the job you want it to—there's no point buying the most gorgeous armchair if it's too narrow to sit in comfortably or looks horrible with the rest of your furniture.

Before visiting a market, make sure you know the dimensions of the room where you intend to place a sofa or armchair. Also, measure the door frame for that room as well as for the front door, and if the room is upstairs, measure the staircase width too. The last thing you want is to take delivery of your sofa but be unable to get it in the house. When shopping, measure the width, height, and length of any pieces that catch your eye, and include any decoration that may stick out, to see if they are the right size. Remember, you won't be able to take a flea-market purchase back.

When buying any kind of secondhand sofa or armchair, always ask yourself whether it's structurally sound and comfortable. If it isn't, how easy would it be to get it repaired and how much is it likely to cost? Always turn a piece over and check the framework for any damage or alterations, which may affect your wish to buy and have an impact on the price you are willing to pay. Getting the frame repaired can be costly and not always worth it.

You may have a picture in your mind of the kind of chair you need. If you don't find what you are looking for, ask around. Dealers probably won't have all their stock on display, and one may have exactly what you are after in their warehouse. Quite often, they will arrange to meet up with you later or send you a picture of the piece, so you can see it for yourself.

ABOVE These sections from a 1970s-style modular seating unit upholstered in wool were on sale at the Round Top Antiques Fair in Texas. Providing the styling are two rather disconcerting china dolls. In the foreground, a pair of occasional chairs from the 1930s in floral upholstery.

OPPOSITE A 1930s French leather sofa, in excellent condition, displayed on a brushed-steel, six-drawer desk from the 1950s, at the Avignon Antiques Fair in southeastern France. To keep your leather furniture in good condition, clean it regularly with saddle soap or a leather cleaner, always mop up spills (leather isn't quite as durable as you may imagine), or even use a vacuum cleaner to remove dust.

ABOVE This two-seater Scandinavian sofa was spotted at the Round Top Antiques Fair in Texas. The leather, particularly on the seats, has become soft and worn over time, which has only added to the sofa's appeal. However, to improve the lifespan of the seat cushions, treat them with some leather conditioner (the pale, worn parts will darken with regular "feeding"). Leaning against the wall behind are some planks of aged wood—more likely old shelves as they have curved edges—ideal for turning into a table or a shelving unit. Propped up against the wall are some colorful vintage cardboard posters.

Always examine any furniture closely for active woodworm before you buy. The woodworm is active when beetle eggs hatch and burrow through cracks in the wood—the tell-tale signs of this are fresh wood dust below the piece of furniture (but this will only be noticeable if the furniture has been standing in one place for a while, which is not always the case at a flea market). Also look for fresh holes where the wood has a pale, clean-edged appearance.

During my recent conversations with dealers, it became clear that they hardly ever restore sofas and armchairs these days because their customers are looking for authenticity. For example, French original wood-framed armchairs, where the covers have been removed to expose the horsehair and burlap (hessian) lining, are very fashionable; the worn gilt of a Louis XV chair is highly desirable; and the wear-and-tear markings of an old leather club chair are absolute prerequisites.

It's rare to find fabric-covered chairs and sofas in immaculate condition. They will often need cleaning, sometimes reupholstering, so be aware of how much this might cost. The average sofa will require

ABOVE A tall, painted, country-style cupboard from France forms the backdrop to the soft leather Danish recliner on its tubular chrome frame. The recliner, from around 1930, is displayed to great advantage high up on a table at the Round Top Antiques Fair in Texas. Even though these two pieces are from different eras and in different design styles, they would complement each other very well in a neutral setting.

RIGHT A Danish flag is draped behind a beautiful Swedish recliner, also at the Round Top Antiques Fair, Texas. Made from woven canvas with a bentwood frame, it was designed in the 1930s and is in spectacular condition. Canvas can be difficult to clean, but dirty marks and dusty crevices can be gently cleaned with warm soapy suds and an old toothbrush.

ABOVE Sculptural, rattan, mid-century chairs, on a single metal stem, curved to add balance. This really great find at the Round Top Antiques Fair, Texas, was brought in by one of the many European traders who sell there. Be wary of buying rattan furniture which is not in decent condition as rattan is difficult to repair.

RIGHT The well-aged concrete wall adds great atmosphere to this scene at Big Daddy's Antiques in San Francisco. Big reproduction metal letters (see chapter 2 for more information) are a really personal decorative touch standing on top of the grand marble fire surround, a fitting backdrop to the two blood-red velvet armchairs, both of them in fantastic condition, which is quite rare to find. The calico-covered sofa on the right can either be left in its current state or reupholstered in a fabric of your choice. The space-saving stack of vintage tables and a chair is like a sculpture.

ABOVE Row upon row of similarly shaped 1950s upholstered dining chairs. They make an impressive display and all are in good condition. When faced with such a choice, you really can cherry pick the best ones. If I were buying, I'd choose a selection in different fabrics and finishes.

about 15 yards (15 meters) of fabric if reupholstered. Add this to the cost of the sofa itself and the reupholstering charges (unless you can do this yourself), and you may end up spending a lot more than you originally intended. But when you discover a rare piece with a fabulous shape, it could just be worth it!

It is always preferable to buy a known name or brand, to guarantee quality, and you will often find that old sofas are better made than some contemporary brands. Frames in beechwood that are dowelled and screwed indicate a quality, long-lasting construction. Likewise, feather-filled seats, although these may have seen better days and need refilling. Stained, turned legs can be changed with little effort (replacement sofa legs are easy to obtain from furniture websites). Don't be put off by scratches—they are easy to fix. There are kits readily available for repairing and restoring minor damage to wood. As long as you get the wood stain in the right color, the results will be stunning. However, if the scratch is more of a gouge, it will need filling with wood filling, then sanding.

Don't feel that you should restrict yourself to a particular period or style of furniture. Instead, focus on what you like. There's no reason why you shouldn't mix and match. If you have a particular make of sofa or chair in mind, learning a little about it in advance is always worthwhile. It will help you to decide whether a piece is a good example of its type and also to know whether the price you are quoted is a fair one.

Vintage furniture usually means 30 or 40 years old, whereas real antique furniture is over 100 years old, but the terms are used loosely. The trend nowadays is for vintage or what we call "preloved"—the best form of

RIGHT Slatted metal folding garden chairs make very useful spare seating (to use indoors or out) as they can be folded and easily stored.

recycling. Mid-century modern sofas and chairs, from the 1930s through to the 1960s, are becoming increasingly popular. G Plan is one example of well-made British furniture from the 1950s that can be found readily at flea markets and on eBay. Designed originally for functional family use, G Plan furniture has become quite iconic, and a viable and more affordable alternative to many Scandinavian designs.

DINING CHAIRS

Finding a set of matching chairs isn't easy but, in any case, it has become fashionable to mix styles, wood finishes, and colors around a dining table. Choosing a period or style of chair that you like—whether country, decorative French, or mid-century modern—will focus your search. The fact that the chairs may not match is irrelevant. Vintage chairs can be smaller than more recent designs, so be sure to test them out against the height of your table.

My friend Rachel Ashwell, who buys many flea-market chairs for her Shabby Chic Couture stores, told me what she looks for when shopping for dining chairs. She is initially always attracted by the patina of a paint finish because of the character it gives. She likes decorative finishes but will avoid a chair if it's fragile or damaged. If cane seats are ripped, though, she would consider replacing them with board and cushions. Woodworm is always a concern with vintage furniture, and if she spots tiny holes and evidence of wood dust, she would not purchase.

ABOVE A pair of reproduction Louis XV dining chairs on sale at Round Top Antiques Fair, Texas. They are upholstered in white calico, with a print of the two halves of a dachsund extending across both chair backs, adding an amusing touch.

RIGHT This design of school chair was really popular in the 1950s and 1960s. They come in multiples, which is great news if you need a matching set. Make sure that chairs like these are the height you want—smaller chairs were often made for very young children as well. Some designs were made from beechwood, so watch out for splinters or cracks.

OPPOSITE A stack of old school chairs in veneered bechwood, from the 1950s/1960s, stenciled with a Union Jack. Beautifully worn and full of character, they are shown here at Big Daddy's Antiques in San Francisco.

LEFT While doing my research for this book in Texas, I stayed with Rachel Ashwell at The Prairie, her gorgeous bed-and-breakfast in Round Top. A seasoned treasure hunter, Rachel has here stored her most recent finds in the barn, ready to be shipped to her Shabby Chic Couture stores. The chairs range in style from basic and plain kitchen chairs to intricate and decorative dining chairs, but each one has been chosen for its patina and character.

BELOW LEFT Original French Tolix Chairs are hard to find and often very expensive but these glossy cherry-red reproductions are a good second-best and very fashionable. They introduce a lively splash of color and suit the industrial look perfectly.

BELOW A trio of Spanish Chairs by the Danish furniture designer Børge Mogensen. These beautiful, oak-framed mid-century chairs, with their tan leather seats and backs, have a strong rustic appearance, highlighted here by being displayed on a large French country dining table. The surrounding dining chairs have rattan seats and plain spindle backs.

TABLES

I LOVE SHOPPING FOR TABLES, AND I HAVE THE INSTINCTIVE ABILITY TO ENVISAGE ANY ONE OF THEM IN SITU, WITH CHAIRS SURROUNDING IT AND EVEN A PITCHER OF FLOWERS IN THE CENTER. CASUAL DINING HAS BECOME THE NORM THESE DAYS, AND THE TABLE AT WHICH WE EAT IS THE HEART OF THE HOME. BUT THE DINING TABLE IS MUCH MORE THAN THAT.

When shopping, have a picture of your ideal table in your head, know the exact size it should be, and, above all, be clear about what it will be used for. You will know you have found the right one when all criteria have been met.

Older tables are usually preferable. They are likely to have been made by hand, generally by a craftsman or artisan. Unless a table is to be used purely decoratively and will not be supporting any weight, it must be sturdy without any wobbles, and with all the legs standing firmly and evenly on the ground. As with all wooden pieces of furniture, check for woodworm, scratches and any more serious damage, and any alterations (see page 20). If one of the legs looks different, which is not unusual, it may have been replaced at a later date, which will lower the value of the table.

As well as the wooden tables you will find in large quantities, you will see Formica-topped tables from the 1950s, as seen in old diners. Look for damp or warped wood, as this means the Formica will peel off.

Old metal tables, that would have once been used in industry, make great desks and can fetch a high price. They will often be painted, but once stripped back and varnished, they will be very desirable.

You will pay a premium if the table is in good condition, but if there is work to be done, you will be in a strong position to negotiate. However, that is only worthwhile if you think you can do the work. The plainer the table, the more likely it is that any repairs will be straightforward to do. An old, polished wooden table that is battered, scratched or stained may benefit from professional French polishing.

Getting a table home can be a challenge, so check if the dealer delivers. Alternatively, make arrangements before your trip—you should be able to find a transporter at the flea market, so look at the market's website in advance.

RIGHT Round, metal, French cafe tables, some with decorated legs and some plain. The tables without a central hole for an umbrella are older than those with a hole. If you wish, you can rub them down and repaint, using an outdoor paint. However, I like to use them as they are indoors, and think that the original patina adds to their character.

BELOW The scene inside the barn at Rachel Ashwell's bed and breakfast, The Prairie, at Round Top in Texas, during the market. Rachel spends many weeks there with her team, treasure-hunting for the specific style of furniture suited to her Shabby Chic Couture business.

STORAGE

CUPBOARDS, CABINETS, CHESTS OF DRAWERS, BEDSIDE TABLES,
NIGHTSTANDS, AND KITCHEN DRESSERS—THESE ARE PROBABLY THE MOST
POPULAR ITEMS TO PASS HANDS AT FLEA MARKETS. MOST HOMES ARE IN
NEED OF MORE STORAGE, AND FLEA MARKETS OFFER THE OPPORTUNITY
TO FIND UNUSUAL AND QUIRKY STORAGE SOLUTIONS.

ABOVE Lined up in Rachel Ashwell's barn on The Prairie ranch is a selection of her finds. At the back are wardrobes and chests and at the foreground is a selection of old tin baby baths. Nowadays these can have so many uses and can be used in the bathroom or kitchen for storage, or as planters in the garden.

OPPOSITE ABOVE A selection of heavily decorated reproduction French-style furniture. It is easy to tell if a piece is reproduction by looking at the interior. New pieces will have clean, undamaged wood, with no blemishes or irregularities. There are many good-quality reproduction pieces to be found at markets—there's nothing wrong with this, but you need to be aware of whether you are buying an antique original or a newer piece, and pay the appropriate price.

As when buying any large piece of furniture, know the measurements of the room and relevant doorframes before you go shopping, and carefully measure any bulky pieces that you consider buying (see page 18). You must be absolutely confident that a dresser, for example, is not too tall for your kitchen and that it will fit not only in its allotted space but also through any doors or windows or around any corners when it's delivered.

The style and shape of large pieces are dependent on your home and your taste. Currently the most popular style, especially for bedrooms, is Louis XV—specifically armoires—for which you can expect to pay premium prices. For your kitchen, you may want something large and imposing. Pine is a good bet, solid and durable, but as antique pine is fashionable, it also carries a high price tag. However, unpainted pine is less sought-after and cheaper. You can easily paint it yourself, in exactly the color and finish you want.

Look for well-made storage. It should be sturdy, and drawers need to run smoothly. Avoid pieces made with inferior materials or where workmanship looks poor—just because a piece is old doesn't mean it is good quality. On the whole, shopping for vintage furniture is a matter of buying what you like, but you may want to restrict yourself to a certain timeframe, which means you will need to identify the period of pieces you like. One good way of doing this is to remove any drawers and check the dovetailed joints. If they are unevenly spaced, the piece is likely to be handmade, as machine-made joints didn't appear until around 1860. Symmetry in a piece of furniture is a sign that it has been machine-made—a real antique is rarely perfect. Identifying the wood finish will also help you date a piece; shellac was the only finish until Victorian times, when it became more common to use wax, oil, or milk paint (made from milk and lime, without any added pigments).

ABOVE The end of a day's trading. Many of the stalls have packed up at the market in Montpellier, leaving one trader with a few interesting pieces of wooden furniture and an antique print of cherubs.

LEFT Sturdy wooden crates were used by breweries and soft drinks companies up until the early 1980s, when glass bottles began to be replaced by plastic. These crates can be painted and used for storage in the home.

ABOVE On a sunny day in Texas at Round Top market, I came across a fabulous selection of chests and stools, mostly Gustavian in style. The diamond-shaped carving is typical of this Swedish style that dates back to 1770. This collection of furniture is not that old, but I loved it for its simplicity. The giant stone torso is a very impressive piece of art.

Knowing the wood that a piece of furniture is made from is also helpful in identifying its age. This chart marries the most popular historic styles today with the woods that were commonly used at that time. Vendors will be able to help you identify the various woods, and you will soon learn to recognize them yourself.

AMERICAN STYLES

Early Colonial (17th century)
Pine, birch, maple, walnut

Late Colonial (18th century)
Pine, mahogany

Federal (early 19th century)
Mahogany, cherry

Pennsylvania Dutch (late 17th century)
Maple, pine, walnut

Shaker (late 18th century)
Pine, maple

BRITISH STYLES

Queen Anne (early 18th century)
Walnut, cherry, mahogany, maple

Georgian Chippendale
(late 18th century)
Mahogany

Victorian (late 19th century)
Mahogany, walnut, rosewood

RIGHT Wallpapered walls inside Rachel Ashwell's Prairie barn provide the pretty backdrop for a few more of the vintage treasures heading for her Shabby Chic Couture stores, chosen for their patina and character.

The distressed look is not everyone's choice when it comes to buying furniture (I agree that a room can look a little overwhelming if it contains nothing but distressed wood). However, displaying a piece in isolation among the clean lines of a modern home can be really beautiful; the lack of distraction allows you to see the piece for what it is and appreciate the patina and the markings of a life lived. All this adds an enormous amount of character to the piece and value to the customer.

My friend Rachel Ashwell, who owns the wonderful Shabby Chic Couture stores, knows how to get this style exactly right. She is always looking for the perfect patina—exposing the years and the different colors it been painted is something that cannot be easily reproduced.

RIGHT Seen here at the antique market in Avignon, a dealer who specializes in furniture from a certain period. Such specialist dealers are generally very knowledgeable and will be able to tell you the provenance of the piece. Keep their contact details in case you want to ask further questions once you have purchased a piece.

BELOW Rachel Ashwell's team offloading more treasures from Round Top, destined for her Shabby Chic Couture stores.

DOORS AND SHUTTERS

IS YOUR SEARCH FOR AN INSIDE OR AN OUTSIDE DOOR? IF YOU INTEND TO USE AN OLD DOOR TO REPLACE YOUR FRONT DOOR, DO SOME RESEARCH FIRST. FIND OUT HOW ROBUST AND SECURE IT NEEDS TO BE FOR THE ROLE AND WHAT WILL BE ACCEPTABLE TO YOUR HOUSE INSURER. IF YOU LIVE IN AN APARTMENT BLOCK, THERE MAY BE SPECIFIC REGULATIONS ABOUT THE KIND OF DOOR YOU ARE ALLOWED.

Thankfully, you will have much more leeway when it comes to choosing an interior door, although check whether any doors need to be fireproof. Above all, it will be the look that encourages you to buy vintage, so don't settle for anything less than perfect for you.

Replacing glass in a door should be approached in the same way as reglazing a window. It can be very difficult to do it yourself, so—if you really love the door—you could get an estimate from a glazier. However, costs can really mount up by the time you add in transport and skilled labor, so I would pass up on the door. There are specialists who deal in stained glass and if the damage is small, repairs can often be made. Send a photo of the damage to a specialist for an estimate.

It's unlikely that your chosen door will fit its allocated opening exactly, but having those measurements to hand when shopping is crucial. Similarly, measure any potential purchase very carefully—for the height, measure the underside of the exterior trim at the top of the frame to the sill on the floor. Door openings can be made a little bigger or smaller, often quite simply, but you must decide how much you love any new door first before you go down that route.

Most doors will be made from wood, although you may come across the occasional metal one. The obvious benefit of a wooden door is that it can be painted any color you want, or you may want to leave it bare and let the beauty of the wood show through. Do you like the locks and handles or will you want to replace them? Does the lock have a key? Check if there are signs of crumbling wood around the lock or handle—be cautious, as this could be a sign of rot or, indeed woodworm (see page 20).

ABOVE Rows and rows of shutters—a common sight at many French markets and seen here in Avignon. The size is the most important consideration as it is difficult to cut them down, apart from slight shaving. Shutters can be hinged together to make interesting screens, or use them as closet doors.

RIGHT A giant stained barn door used here as a decorative backdrop. With original rusted hinges and old carvings in the wood, this piece has a hidden story. Here it sits above an old cupboard, displaying a variety of decorative objects, including an old storage jar, a small leather case for gentlemen's brushes, and a wooden keepsake box.

ABOVE Pairs of exquisitely beautiful carved doors, leaning against a metal container in a French market. Many doors of this style date back to the seventeenth and eighteenth centuries, and were seen in many French buildings and châteaux. The decorative metal grills in the upper panels can be backed with mirror or glass. These make great internal doors, or a skilled carpenter could build cupboards or closets to fit around them.

SHUTTERS

Shutters usually have a practical purpose—at the window, as a replacement for curtains, to block out the light inside, for security, or as the doors to cupboards and closets.

Flea-market shutters tend to be French, and originally from grand old châteaux. You will often come across a set of them, which is useful, as they will all be the same size and will look lovely used together in your home. Things to look out for are weather damage and peeling paint. Take a look at the wood beneath to check that it is salvageable—it usually is. The cleaning, stripping, and painting that follows will be a labor of love for you, but the end result will be so worth it.

Although you will come across solid panels, some with fretwork patterns, the most common shutters at flea markets are slatted. These are definitely harder to restore, but if you are using them inside your home, they don't need to offer any protection from the elements and so you can leave them looking old and weary, which is so attractive and adds a great deal of character.

For shutters to be used on the outside, it is worth doing a good job on their restoration, sanding them back and applying an undercoat and weather-resistant paint. Remember, these shutters could be a few hundred years old, so there is no reason why they can't last for many more years.

Shutters can also be used for purely decorative purposes in your home or yard. They can bring interest to a bare expanse of wall, perhaps hung with art or accessories, or be left just as they are, with their age showing through the peeling layers of paint.

RIGHT A selection of antique shutters and window frames seen in Texas. Mirrored glass has been added to two of the frames, creating unique decorative pieces for the home.

CHAPTER 2:
WALL ART

VINTAGE SIGNS

THE HISTORY OF SIGNAGE DATES BACK TO ANCIENT TIMES—THE FIRST KNOWN WRITTEN ADVERTISEMENT, DATING FROM 3000 BC, CAN STILL BE SEEN ON RUINS IN THE EGYPTIAN CITY OF THEBES. MODERN-DAY ADVERTISING BEGAN IN THE EARLY EIGHTEENTH CENTURY. WITH THE RISE OF CONSUMERISM, PAINTED WOODEN SIGNS WERE USED TO ADVERTISE STORES AND THE GOODS THEY SOLD.

ABOVE The word "Hope" spelt out at the Round Top Antiques Fair in Texas. The 3D tin letters are reproduction, but because they are starting to rust, they have a very authentic feel.

OPPOSITE A cardboard sign, with an old version of the Pepsi Cola logo, that looks hand-painted, also seen at Round Top. The brown staining from age, and possibly nicotine, gives a clue as to its past—more than likely it once hung in a diner or a bar at Bill's Market.

By 1900, consumerism had increased to such an extent that brand advertising became a very competitive business, particularly in the U.S. Signage was the most effective way of raising a brand's profile and maintaining it. We feature many examples here, and you will find plenty for yourself at markets. They make great funky wall art, especially in the kitchen.

Tin was the natural choice of material for these signs. It doesn't rust easily, so can be left hanging outdoors. Tin signs were actually made of steel coated in tin, and their production coincided with the rise of the steel industry, which meant that it was readily available. However, the use of steel for making anything other than weapons was banned by World War I. Tin signs did make a comeback after the war but, by the 1950s, they had been replaced. Vintage tin signs are very popular today and hold their value well. I have come across a huge number on my travels, advertising anything from Coca-Cola to motor parts and gasoline (petrol).

Porcelain enamel signs took over from tin, an idea that was imported to the U.S. from Germany. The signs were made up of layers of color coated with powdered glass and were fired in an oven, which made them very durable. The first signs were stenciled, but American designers soon switched to silk screens.

These signs are often very colorful and make great decoration for the home, but beware of reproductions—there are many on the market, and some are even found at antique markets. These will be made to look distressed and will almost always be very lightweight. Some signs will be stamped with the date of manufacture. If you are at all uncertain about authenticity, you may need to do some research or simply put your trust in

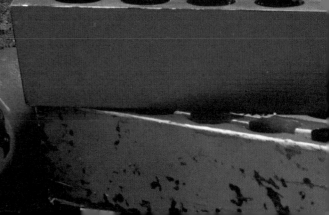

BelAir

FARMALL

36 CHEVROLET APACHE

CHEVROLET

the dealer. A useful tip is that some of the rare porcelain enamel signs still around are from the early drinks companies, advertising the likes of Coca-Cola. From the 1930s, all through the U.S. and Europe, the advertising sign became commonplace.

If you are a collector, spotting the real thing is much easier because you have an eye for it, but if you are looking for a sign to hang on an empty wall, does it really matter whether it is authentic or not? Your choice of sign may well be about its message or color or, indeed, the brand, because it has some significance for you.

Your choice of sign hinges mostly on the suitability of the color or design of the room where you intend to display it. The obvious place is on the wall, but if the sign is made of tin, iron, or steel, it will be very difficult to get it to hang flat without restoring or mending it, which will often affect the graphics or the quality of the paint. The characteristic aging of the sign may have been what attracted you in the first place, so perhaps you should consider whether repair is an option. The sign could just as easily be propped up against the wall and still add something special to the room.

Nostalgic signs have a rare quality in that they awaken memories and remind you of times gone by. Including one or more signs among an arrangement of paintings, sketches, and mirrors will create a strong feature wall in any home.

ABOVE A large industrial fan, no longer in working order, from a factory of some kind, with the emblem of the company shown on the disk in the center. Such a piece would have a massive impact in an industrial-style home, hanging from the rafters in an old warehouse.

OPPOSITE This fabulous selection of American car fender (bumper) plates from the 1950s would make fantastic wall art in a boy's bedroom. I discovered them at Round Top in Texas, but there are plenty to be found all over the U.S.—the car capital of the world.

LEFT A mesh fence, like a folding screen, acts as the backdrop for this selection of enamel signs, which look as though they have come from an industrial machinery or electrical components company. On sale at the Ventura Beach flea market in California, they are accompanied by a random selection of books, tennis rackets, a wooden stepladder, and chairs.

ABOVE A carefully displayed selection of enamel advertising signs, ranging from the Navy & Army Canteen Board sign from the 1920s to a rather modern-looking credit card sign. Signs like these —some battered, some iconic—are often found at markets, advertising various products and services, as well as issuing warnings.

LEFT It was a surprise to see these London Underground subway signs so far from home, at Round Top, Texas. It wasn't quite so surprising when we realized the vendor was English, married to an American. His stock was a very eclectic mix, expertly sourced from across two continents. Shopping from vendors recommended to you by seasoned shoppers can reap dividends.

OPPOSITE The Bennett's Ice Cream sign is likely to be 40–50 years old. The very rusty chairs behind could be restored by rubbing them down and powder-coating or painting them with a suitable metal paint. On the other hand, you might wish to buy them simply for their character.

ILLUMINATED SIGNS

The first electrical sign was seen in London during the International Electrical Exposition in January 1892 in London. Emblazoned across it with incandescent bulbs was the name "Edison," its American inventor. The U.S. continued to pioneer outdoor light display, and by the early 1900s the electric sign was seen across the country, with retail businesses recognizing what this form of advertsing could do for their them.

It was a French scientist who developed a way of liquefying neon gas, and discovered it was sensitive to electrical charge and produced a bright light. A further discovery was that a drop of mercury added to the neon gas produced a bright blue color. This was the birth of the neon tube, which could be molded into different shapes. By 1922 the first neon sign was imported into the U.S., where it quickly became a prolific advertising medium.

There is something very rock'n'roll about electrical or neon signage, and nothing quite like a neon sign to evoke the razzle-dazzle of Las Vegas at night. It has a slightly racy, even provocative image, and it is an excellent way of creating real drama in a room.

When buying vintage illuminated signs, you must have a qualified electrician check them over before using. Not only will there be bulbs missing but they could also need some new wiring, which you should never do yourself. If repairs are needed to the lights themselves, be aware that glass benders and neon repairers are hard to find, although not impossible.

LEFT Seen in Texas, this giant illuminated arrow would probably have once identified the entrance to a bar or club.

ABOVE This giant chop suey restaurant sign, mounted on a metal mesh, would make a fun piece of wall art for a kitchen.

ABOVE Giant letters spelling out "eat" is an open invitation to buy for someone who wants to bring some industrial chic into their domestic kitchen, or, indeed, a bar.

BELOW RIGHT A jumble of oversized rusty letters, seen here at a flea market in Avignon, France, reflected in a large gilt mirror. Traders will often acquire an odd selection of letters as they clear homes, factories, and so on, and never knowing what you might discover at a flea market is one of the great pleasures of treasure hunting.

INDIVIDUAL LETTERS

The current popularity of all things personalized and custom-made has seen a surge in interest for salvaged letters that once formed part of old advertising billboards and street or theater signs. Collecting the letters of a loved one's name or their initials in different shapes, sizes, or colors can make a touching and thoughtful gift, as well as adding a really unusual and unique design element to a room. Smaller letters can be propped up on a shelf or mantelpiece or hung from hooks on the wall. Larger ones, meanwhile, can be stood against a wall, creating instant impact.

Most vintage signs are made up of one word or a short slogan or saying. However, they do often come as individual letters, and end up at flea markets. Increasingly, though, savvy vendors are now selling reproduction letters—in metal, plastic, and 3D—all meeting consumer demand.

Many times I have rummaged through a whole pile of letters desperately searching for the most popular ones, and therefore the most versatile, trying to create a particular word, or for the letters of a friend's name. But, since these letters were never produced to sell individually, they have become quite rare and I often come away disappointed.

Illuminated light boxes were very popular in the 1950s and '60s (see page 51). They were used as large-scale menus in restaurants, with the slot-in letters easy to change according to the meals being served. Movie theaters also used them to advertise current and future screenings. Rarely

seen now as they were intended, these light boxes have produced a lot of single letters, which are commonplace at markets, usually in black and a simple font.

Light-up letters are rare but if you're lucky enough to find any, as with anything electrical, check to see that they are in working order and make sure a qualified electrician checks them over before you use them.

The range of letter styles you come across is quite astonishing. While shopping at Round Top Antiques Market in Texas, we came across lots of Depression-era signage from the 1930s. These were mostly black letters, enameled or made from cast aluminum. We also saw a number of letters that were single-sided and die-cut, often in bright primary colors, some with beveled edges. These would have come from bowling alleys, electrical companies, or motor showrooms. By the 1940s and '50s, the signage was produced in 3D, with folded and pressed steel. Most of these types of letters would have been removed from building façades.

Wherever you can, try to find out the provenance and history of the letters. Knowing their past brings them to life, and it is this that makes the hunt for your treasures, whatever they are, even more rewarding.

TOP A fabulous selection of bold, colored letters in a font style that suggests mid-century. They would have been backlit originally and need some electrical work to get them working again. But even as they are, they would still make unusual and attractive decorations.

ABOVE A wall of elongated letters, most likely from the 1940s, seen here at an antiques market in Isle-sur-la-Sorgue, in Provence.

RIGHT These letters, also found at Round Top, spell out "Goodyear," as in the car tires. The painted vintage "76" sign once advertised a chain of gas stations. When buying letters, think about the order in which to display them. These, for example, could stay the way are and make a wacky New Year greeting. Alternatively, rearrange letters to your heart's content, devising various anagrams and messages.

LEFT A field full of giant 3D letters at Round Top in Texas. Made from tin, they now have a rather rusty appearance, giving them all the more character—great for displaying outdoors in a large yard or as a store sign, or in a bar or café.

BELOW I suspect that these letters, forming the word "owl," once spelt "bowl" and were mounted outside a bowling alley, long since gone.

PAINTINGS AND PORTRAITS

BUYING ART IS VERY SUBJECTIVE, TOTALLY PERSONAL, AND INCREDIBLY DIFFICULT TO DO FOR SOMEONE ELSE. TO HAVE A PIECE OF ART HANGING IN YOUR HOME, TO LOOK AT IT EVERY DAY, YOU MUST LOVE IT. FOCUSING ON CERTAIN IMAGES OR THEMES—SEASCAPES, FLOWERS, OR PORTRAITS—CAN BE FUN WHEN COLLECTING, AND IT ALSO MAKES THE HUNT EASIER.

BUYING ART

One thing people often want to know is how to tell the age of a painting. You can start with the color of the canvas. The darker it looks, the older it is— white canvas has only been used since the 1980s. Checking the wood that the canvas is stretched over can also provide a clue, as can the nails. Again, the darker the wood, the older the painting. However, there is a catch. It could be that the painting has at some point been removed from its original stretcher if it needed repairing and then restretched on lighter-colored wood. All very frustrating, I know, because it doesn't really solve the issue. However, does the age of a painting really matter? As I've said many times, if you like it and it represents value for money for you, then buy it.

Vintage art is unlikely to be in perfect condition, and deciding if any wear or tear matters enough to stop you buying a piece is a personal thing and entirely up to you. You may find that the oil paint is cracked—the word for the fine crazing is "craquelure," which is a sign of nothing more serious than that the varnish has shrunk. Or you could discover a small tear in the canvas, which, of course, can be restored—there are many experts out there—but, as with all these specialty skills, it comes at a cost. You may decide either not to buy the piece or to embrace its imperfections.

It is good to know if a painting is an oil or a print. The simple test is to check for brush strokes. Touch the piece with your finger to feel the texture, but wipe your finger first—oil residue on the skin can cause damage. Most flea market vendors won't mind you doing this but never try it in a gallery! You may come across prints with a shellac coating, to give the appearance of an oil painting—manufacturers like to mimic old art—so beware.

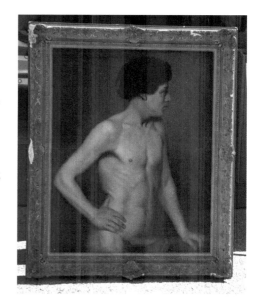

ABOVE A typical example of the art found at a Côte d'Azur flea market in southwest France, this male nude oil painting on canvas is displayed in a rather chipped but decorative gilt frame. Minor damage to gilt like this can easily be repaired but if it doesn't spoil your enjoyment of a piece, there's really no reason to bother.

ABOVE The style and character of the double portrait, as well as of the frame, indicate that it is from the 1940s or '50s.

LEFT A jumble of art seen here at an English country flea market—mainly prints in repro frames and most likely from house clearances. The paintings could be hung as they are or the paintings could be thrown away, leaving you with a frame that is a piece of art in its own right.

ABOVE This symphony in brown, with a distinct 1940s feel to the painting, shows how appealing an apparently haphazard display using an old, battered door can be.

LEFT Large, diverse displays like this, inside one of the big halls at the Montpellier Antiques Market in southwestern France, can help you decide what you are looking for. Classic oils on canvas, both portraits and landscapes, in ornate gilded frames lie alongside modern abstract art from the 1960s.

There's no doubt that oil painting has been the most popular form of painting over the last 500 years, and it continues to be so. Painting in oils is taught widely in art colleges and schools, and it is a highly respected skill. Oils are more valuable generally than acrylics or watercolors, which are usually sold under glass. The colors in oils tend to be richer and deeper.

Some paintings may come with a certificate of authenticity, which confirms that the piece is what the seller says it is. Or the painting may have a provenance, which is a record of ownership and leaves you in no doubt that a piece is genuine. If a seller gives you the name of the artist, it is very easy to confirm quickly online.

There are always many art school paintings for sale at flea markets, especially portraits that have been painted during art classes. A friend of mine is an avid collector of portraits. She has hung them all together, unframed, up a stairwell and the effect is very impressive.

When searching for paintings to feature in this book, we knew we didn't want smiling faces, but we didn't want menacing ones either! That's perhaps something to bear in mind—you need faces you can happily live with!

BELOW The style of portraiture and the clothes worn by the sitter can be an indication of the age of a painting. Found at a French flea market, this unframed oil on canvas shows a rather serious-looking man with a thick mustache, a look that was very popular around the early 1900s.

ABOVE A decorated gilt frame surrounds the photograph of a young Russian soldier. Some heavy leather army boots continue the military theme, although the two crystal chandeliers reinforce the randomness of this display of vintage goods at a flea market in Montpellier in southern France.

LEFT A Victorian birdcage made of wood and wire. These are becoming increasingly difficult to find, especially if they are in good condition. This one is in excellent shape and would fetch a relatively high price. The clothes and hairstyle of the sitter in the unframed oil on canvas suggest the portrait was painted in the 1940s or '50s.

OPPOSITE Although the items in this well-considered display of antiques are more than likely European, they were spotted at Round Top Antiques Market in Texas. When treasure hunting, always look beyond the original role of a piece and imagine how you could use it as something else. Vintage and battered luggage, like this old suitcase, make great bedside tables, perhaps one piled up on another. If you don't like the picture in a frame, could you use the frame on its own?

BELOW Whether displayed on a rather shabby, retro, upholstered chair, as here, or on the wall, these three pretty pictures go so well together, linked by their size and simple gold frames.

BELOW RIGHT A damaged frame should not necessarily put you off making a purchase. Although the gilt frame of this oil on canvas, depicting a gentleman in period costume, is very distressed, it would be easy to get repaired or you could simply touch it up with gilt paint yourself.

Even if you discover that a painting you like is not an original but a print, you should not automatically dismiss it for that reason alone. However, you should ask yourself whether it is a limited edition. This is a sign of rarity and adds to the reasons for buying. The print should bear the artist's signature and a number indicating how many prints were made and where it comes in the hierarchy. For example, 12/100 indicates that this is the 12th print out of 100. The lower the number of the print, the better the buy. You can also check if there is a sticker from the printing company on the back of the print. From this, you can research which artists they represented and when, and possibly even find the person who created the original artwork.

Before embarking on your art treasure hunt, be clear about what you like. If you're unsure, visit your local gallery or museum and look at lots of styles and educate yourself on technique, color, style, and theme. Armed with this information and knowing what you like will give you an enormous amount of confidence when shopping. For instance, I'm a huge fan of the 1912–40 Bloomsbury Set, particularly the paintings of Duncan Grant and Vanessa Bell (Virginia Woolf's sister). Although I can't afford the originals, many of these artists' contemporaries were influenced by their style. And I am lucky to have found some of their work and bought it.

Over the years, I have collected pictures with flower themes, black-and-white pictures… the list is endless. But I always end up giving most of them to friends or put them away as I love to change things around.

MOVIE MEMORABILIA

Movie posters have always been popular flea-market buys. The film industry has produced some amazing artwork over the years, which has been used in movie theaters across the world, as well as on billboards, in subways, and so on. I have seen many examples on my flea-market travels, but the most impressive selection was at Round Top in Texas, which isn't that surprising, as the U.S. is the home of the movie industry.

The condition of the poster and the age of the movie dictate the price. Original posters are rare. By original, I mean a poster that was produced by the studio to advertise the movie at the theater for its first release. Posters more than 30 years old would have been produced using genuine illustrated artwork, and the brush strokes would be apparent—photographic layouts or computer-generated images were a thing of the future.

The re-release of a film usually comes with a new poster produced by the studio, which is also very collectible. Of much less value are reproduction posters. These are printed for their aesthetic and commercial qualities only, not for promoting a movie.

Other movie memorabilia includes old theater seats, and I have bought and sold a great many in my time. There is always enormous demand for them and, as a result, they usually fetch a high price, but bear in mind that their quality does vary enormously. Illuminated clocks and light boxes (see page 52) make great nostalgic pieces but get a qualified electrician to check they are safe to use. You may also come across popcorn machines but, in my experience, they will be reproductions—original machines are very rare.

LEFT Inside at Round Top, Texas, interesting old movie and music hall pictures and posters decorate these walls. Posters of Westerns are particular favorites here. Although the old carved bed and chandelier are unlikely companions for the posters, this attractive display shows that mixing up styles and eras can make for the most distinctive and interesting interior.

ABOVE It's not always possible to identify a flea-market find, and this big illustrated poster, in rather garish colors, is a case in point. The sheer size of the poster, however, suggests it could be a movie star. Together with the neon sign, in working order, fireman's hat, and an old takeout pizzeria sign, it evokes a nostalgic image of vintage Americana.

MIRRORS & FRAMES

VINTAGE OR VINTAGE-STYLE MIRRORS ARE VERY SOUGHT-AFTER, AND RIGHTLY SO. THEY CAN TRANSFORM ANY ROOM AND CERTAINLY SHOULDN'T BE RESTRICTED TO BATHROOMS AND BEDROOMS. IN THESE ROOMS, THEY HAVE A PRACTICAL ROLE, SO YOU MAY WISH TO HAVE THE GLASS RESILVERED OR EVEN REPLACED.

ABOVE Mirrors have more to offer than just reflections. At this Avignon market, an oval mirror in an ornate frame doubles up as a tray for a pair of metal soap dishes that are rusty with age.

OPPOSITE A selection of old mirrors, nicely distressed and from different periods. The empty but decorative metal frame at the front could be refitted with a mirror or just hung as it is. The two wood-framed mirrors behind have been newly painted and rubbed down to give a vintage feel, while the plain framed mirror shows its age with its spotted glass.

However, in other rooms of the house, where mirrors don't need to offer a good reflection, re-silvering isn't necessary. I actually really like the effect of black spotting (also called foxing) on a mirror—it has a mysterious, romantic quality.

Sometimes it's worth buying a mirror for the frame alone. Romantic French mirrors placed above a small, white-painted table can create a wonderful boudoir feel, while a large, black-framed mirror in a simple style above a fireplace will add a sense of drama. Hanging a mirror in a dark, narrow hall or room will increase the sense of light as well as space, while an oversized Louis XV-style mirror leaning against a wall in a modern home will look both stunning and original. Mixing styles like this is a clever way to create a home that is uniquely yours.

The idea of framing pictures goes back as far as the 1300s, when paintings in churches were framed and often resembled windows or arches. This "gothic" style caught on, and framed pictures soon appeared in the homes of the wealthy. By 1690, the most important city for frame-making was Paris, where the frames were all carved and assembled by furniture-makers—an indication of how important they were considered to be at the time. As the centuries progressed, the frames changed in style, always mirroring the prevalent styles of furniture.

Empty vintage and original frames are always in plentiful supply at markets, when the art has long been discarded or destroyed but has left behind a fabulous frame. If the frame is wooden, make sure that you check for woodworm and rot (see page 20).

The most popular frames today are from the Victorian era, particularly the late 1800s. They are usually very ornate and thick, and made of gesso. The thicker and heavier the frame, the more valuable it is. Inevitably with old frames, there will be chips, typically on the corners. These usually don't stop me buying a frame because the chips add so much character. However, there definitely comes a time when the chipping has gone too far and it will require too much investment, in time and money, to restore the frame.

In French flea markets, you will come across a wealth of decorative frames, from both paintings and mirrors. The Louis XV period in the eighteenth century is particularly desirable and popular. Private individuals often buy them to paint and restore themselves. Whitewashing a frame and putting a new mirror in to hang in a bathroom looks sensational.

If the ostentation of Louis XV frames is too much for you, you are probably best advised to search for art deco pieces from the 1930s, with their clean lines and minimal decoration. Instead of curves and gilt, you are likely to be presented with straight sides and darker wood.

TOP Mirrors that do not vie for attention, like these from the 1950s, benefit from being hung in a group to create a feature wall. Modern mirrors are easy to come by in flea markets. These are appropriately displayed with a hairdresser's chair in the foreground.

OPPOSITE The paintwork of this mirror, with its elaborate pediment, has been distressed, which suggests that the mirror is Louis XV-style, not an original. Nevertheless, it is a very attractive shape that is worth repainting or regilding.

ABOVE If you go to a flea market looking for a mirror, this is just the kind of vendor you would wish to buy from: he specializes in mirrors, has a varied selection, and is careful that the quality of his stock is good.

LEFT A treasure-trove of gilt frames in excellent condition, most without their art. When hunting for gilt frames, check for cracks, chips, and missing pieces—these will all reduce the price.

BELOW This is a particularly beautiful gilt frame, with very intricate detailing. Gently cleaning with a toothbrush and warm water, in case there are any loose carvings, will prolong its good looks.

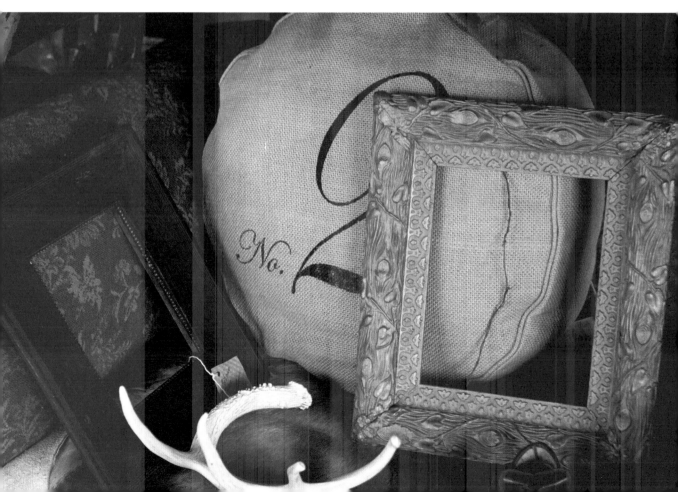

ABOVE Judging by this selection of aged vintage pieces at a big outdoor market in the English countryside, the vendor is likely to be from France or Belgium. In among the garden pots, a shelf unit made of thread spools (cotton reels), and metal garden tables and chairs is a selection of vintage wooden frames. These would be perfect for fitting with mirror glass.

LEFT A cart full of gilt-framed pictures—some old, some reproduction. Identifying which is which can be done by the color of the canvas, the framer's label, or the artist's name. An established vendor might also be able to advise.

CHINA

COLLECTING CHINA CAN BE ADDICTIVE, BUT THE FASHIONS COME AND GO. TEN YEARS AGO, I WAS A KEEN COLLECTOR OF TEA CUPS AND SAUCERS WITH PRETTY FLORAL DECORATIONS, FROM EARLY ENGLISH STAFFORDSHIRE POTTERY, SPODE, AND WEDGWOOD TO FRENCH LIMOGES PORCELAIN. I STILL HAVE THEM, BUT THEY'RE IN A CUPBOARD. NOW THE FASHION IS FOR ROBUST, WHITE EARTHENWARE.

EARTHENWARE

Earthenware is made of baked clay. It is much coarser and more porous than ceramics because it is fired at a much lower temperature and not for as long. To help overcome its porosity, earthenware is almost always glazed.

You will find many examples of unglazed earthenware in flea markets around the world. Easily recognizable by its brownish-orange color, it is most often used for pitchers, pots, and bowls. It has a casual rustic feel and was particularly popular during the 1980s. Creamware is a much finer, cream-colored version of earthenware, created in 1750 in Staffordshire, England. Josiah Wedgwood, with his partner Thomas Whieldon, was the best-known producer of creamware, which was sold under the name of pearlware.

The best way to clean earthenware is in the dishwasher on a gentle cycle. For stubborn stains, try soaking the piece in a gallon of water with a cup of ammonia. Don't use a heavy scourer, as this can damage the glaze.

OPPOSITE ABOVE An impressive selection of very sought-after white porcelain pedestal cake stands, all in excellent condition. You will generally find a metal screw through the middle of such stands, to stabilize them.

RIGHT I came across this amazing array of white porcelain at the French antiques market in Avignon. It may well have been a sale of hotel or restaurant stock, although this is often identified by a stamp of the establishment on the bottom of the piece, but, in this instance, there was none.

ABOVE These serving platters on a stand at Round Top Antiques Market in Texas are almost certainly from the early 1900s—a telltale sign is the absence of any stamp on the underneath. Once used at banquets in grand houses, they are now commonplace in antique and flea markets. It is quite easy to find pieces in good condition, partly because there is not a great demand for them these days.

CERAMICWARE

Stoke-on-Trent, England, was the heart of the china industry back in 1740, having grown from a strong base of clay mining. Known as The Potteries, the area stretched over a 12-mile radius of North Staffordshire. You will find china from Stoke-on-Trent in flea markets all over the world. I saw many examples in both Texas and Los Angeles during my research for this book. In French markets, you are more likely to come across porcelain made with clay from the city of Limoges. Production started back in 1770, and the Limoges name continues to represent the premier manufacturing city in France. Many private factories, including Havilland and Bernardaud, used the famous Limoges clay and still do to this day.

The china you choose to collect is very much a question of personal preference. When I started out, I was interested in Royal Staffordshire and Royal Doulton, partly because it was widely available and easy to put together collections in the same pattern. Occasionally, though, I would branch out and find something a little special, such as some beautiful plates of Limoges clay, made by Haviland of France, which I still treasure.

ABOVE The vendor at Round Top took the time to create a really well-thought-out wall display of individual plates, linked by their heavily decorated patterns in similar colors. In among them, there is likely to be at least one piece from the Staffordshire potters of Johnson Brothers. Their china, particularly designs featuring rustic scenes, was popular in the U.S. at the end of the nineteenth century for its durability and low cost.

RIGHT A cake stand, which looks to be either early Spode or Wedgwood, with an intricate blue pattern, on sale at Kempton Park market, in the south of England. The piece isn't in perfect condition—you can see a chip in the upper rim —but for me that gives it a history and makes it more interesting.

Back in the mid-1980s, I started collecting chintzware—china decorated in a colorful pattern resembling chintz fabric—which was great fun and also easy because there was a lot of it about, unlike today. Producing chintzware was a highly competitive business in the twentieth century.

If you decide to collect a certain pattern, there are many china-matching websites out there, but you can make more of a statement if your collection is by theme or color, perhaps mixing blues, floral Delftware, and striped Cornishware, or pinks, reds, florals, and spots. The eclectic tea party look of jumbled patterns is for me quite special. Having two different patterns for a cup and saucer looks wonderful, or mixing a plain saucer with a floral cup.

When buying china, it makes sense to check if there are any repairs. These are often an indication that the piece won't stand up to regular use, but if you're intending to use it for display only, and the repairs don't spoil your enjoyment of it, there's no reason not to buy.

Broken china is also worth considering. You may be able to repair it quite easily by gluing the pieces together, as long as there aren't too many of them. Before buying, though, put the pieces together to make sure they do actually fit and that there aren't any missing. When you get the item home, clean it thoroughly first—household acetone is probably best—and then run glue along one edge, wait a few seconds until tacky, and then press together. I find that the best glue for this is an epoxy resin, which usually comes in two tubes. The piece won't last as long as something that hasn't been repaired, but if it means saving your favorite china or giving you back a full set, it is well worth it.

LEFT Stacks of china bowls, platters, and plates in blue and white designs. Although from a range of ceramic and porcelain houses, the display proves that mixing styles and patterns works really well, as long as there is a linking theme.

ABOVE A pleasing jumble of designs in a wooden plate rack, some more familiar than others, such as the typical plum design from Royal Worcester. The vintage floral print plate in the foreground is from the Italian company Richard Ginori, and this design is still made today. The company has a full replacement service, which you can use to identify various patterns and the year of manufacture.

As well as being cracked, old pieces of china may be stained. For example, a teapot that has endured years of being filled with boiling water and tea leaves is likely to be crackled and leaky, with ingrained tannin stains. Any stains inside will be not be seen, so there really is not much point trying to get rid of them. However, many can be removed. Spot cleaning with warm water and detergent, mixed with a little household bleach, can do the trick. For more stubborn stains, you can soak the china in hydrogen peroxide for at least an hour. As this is a bleaching agent, test on an area of pattern that is not on plain view, so you don't risk removing all the pattern.

Vintage plates hanging together on the wall make a very attractive and creative display. The easiest way to do this is with a wire plate hanging hook. Alternatively, buy a canvas sticky disc with a hook on it. A word of warning, however: don't use these in a humid room (such as a kitchen or bathroom) because the disc will detach from the plate, which then falls to the floor. I found out the hard way…

Having collected china for more years than I care to remember, I now have a huge big box of vintage cups, saucers, plates, and teapots. Although they're no longer in everyday use or on display, they're not redundant. Redolent of a bygone age, they are always being loaned to friends for a celebration of one kind or another, turning afternoon tea into a glorious ritual.

ABOVE This box of retro china on sale at Round Top came straight out of a house clearance. It is more than likely Mikasa china, dating from around 1960. One of the advantages of collecting china from a huge dinnerware company like Mikasa, which still exists, is that there are many china replacement websites selling its wares, should you wish to match missing items.

BELOW RIGHT A pair of covered serving dishes and a gravy boat. Their clean, modern design indicates they are from the 1950s or 1960s.

OPPOSITE A bowl and pitcher in French country stencilware, together with a soap dish and trinket tray, making up a bedroom or bathroom set. The art deco styling places them from around 1925.

ABOVE A vintage 1940s Burleigh Ware, double-handled vase, made in Staffordshire, England. The distinctive blue-and-white pattern is their Calico design, which is still available today.

LEFT These stoneware retro vases are very easy and cheap to come by. Mostly European, with many from West Germany, from the 1950s and '60s, they are heavy-duty and can be found in a number of different styles.

GLASS

IT WAS DURING MY FLEA-MARKET TRAVELS ACROSS THE U.S., WHICH INCLUDED THE MASSIVE ROUND TOP ANTIQUES MARKET IN TEXAS, AS WELL AS SMALLER FAIRS IN SAN FRANCISCO AND LOS ANGELES, THAT I CAME ACROSS THE MOST FANTASTIC COLLECTIONS OF COLORED GLASSWARE, FROM COMPLETE DINING SETS TO INDIVIDUAL BOWLS, PITCHERS, PLATES, AND GLASSES.

ABOVE Amber Depression glass from the 1960s, seen here at Round Top, Texas. Often seen in blue, pink, green, and lilac as well, this range of American glassware, which was first produced in 1929, is highly collectible.

OPPOSITE ABOVE Rows of pale blue Depression drinking glasses and a rack full of varying shades of blue glass—all desirable and collectible.

OPPOSITE BELOW This green-patterned Depression glass, made mostly in the 1950s and '60s, is highly collectible. Reproduction Depression glass is made today in China but is of a poorer quality and doesn't have the raised seams of the originals.

I discovered Depression glass in colors that ranged from dark blue, amber, and pale pink to green and lilac. Produced by U.S. manufacturers, such as Federal Glass and Anchor Hocking Glass, it was designed in the late 1920s, to bring a little cheer into the everyday lives of people during the Great Depression, when money was tight, jobs were scarce, and so many sacrifices had to be made in the home.

Depression glass was mass-produced very cheaply. The heavy molds weren't always perfect but they were undeniably cheerful and functional. It was often used as a giveaway with purchases of certain groceries, such as cereal or washing powder. Today, it is highly collectible and has a rich history. Even though Depression glass is hardwearing, it is always advisable to wash it—and any other glassware for that matter—by hand and in a plastic bowl to avoid clanking. Warm, soapy water will give the best results.

There are many reproductions of Depression glass now on the market but there are certain things to check to ensure you are looking at the real thing. Since Depression glass was made in molds, it has distinctive raised seams, whereas the reproductions do not. Wavy ripples on the bottom, as a result of the molds aging, are another sign of the real thing. Importantly, take note of what vendors say—they should be able to tell you about the history of Depression glass, and also have an authentic listing of factories that made it, as well as reference images.

Up until the late seventeenth century, the best-quality glassware in Europe came out of Italy. Then British glass began to rival it, thanks to George Ravenscroft, who developed lead glass, which revolutionized glass production. Lead glass was of a much finer quality—less brittle and very clear. Early drinking glasses were hand-blown, so their shapes

can vary enormously, but this is what makes collecting them such a pleasure. I particularly like heavy-bottomed glasses, commonly known as balusters.

Bistro glassware, which I found in great quantity in the French markets of Avignon, Montpellier, and Béziers, is likely to be from old restaurants and bars. I love their chunky shape, and the simplicity and robust nature of the style. Machine-made and dishwasher-proof, this is just the kind of vintage glass for everyday use.

I love old glassware, but appreciate that perfect examples can be difficult to find at flea markets. Inspect it closely for chips, cracks, and staining. Limescale deposits can build up and give the glass a very cloudy effect. You might be able to eradicate this by soaking in one part household ammonia mixed with four parts warm water. Or you could try soaking a single piece in warm water with a teaspoon each of vinegar and salt. For more stubborn stains, try denture cleaner or lemon juice and increase the amount of elbow grease, but don't overdo it—glass by its very nature is fragile. Cleaning narrow-necked bottles and decanters is a little more challenging. Fix a small piece of sponge to the unfurled hook of a coat hanger and push it to the bottom of the piece and rub gently.

BELOW A collection of dinner plates, tea plates, and milk pitchers in green milk glass, known as jadeite. It has a lovely retro feel and is in plentiful supply in U.S. flea markets. Durable and stain-resistant, jadeite was first made in the 1930s.

ABOVE Glassware, particularly for drinking wine and spirits, comes in an incredible range of shapes. In the foreground, from left to right: a dram glass, used for port; a wine glass with a stout stem and quite heavy base; a smaller glass for sherry or liqueurs; a variety of crystal wine glasses. In the background, two Murano boat-shaped vases from the 1960s.

LEFT A set of heavy-bottomed French bistro wine glasses, sturdy and robust, from around 1900. As this style of glassware was used primarily in restaurants and bars, you should expect to find a great number of them in flea markets, particularly in France.

ABOVE A collection of beautiful vivid blue glass demijohns or carboys, which were used for transporting large quantities of wine or spirits from as early as the 1700s. Popular now as statement pieces in modern interiors, you can find them in flea markets in a range of sizes.

RIGHT The uneven shape of this clear glass demijohn indicates that it is hand-blown and therefore quite old, possibly as early as the 1700s. These early demijohns are particularly collectible.

OPPOSITE BELOW The visible seams on these very round demijohns indicate that they have been made from a mold. The attractive, stuck-on paper labels depict the branding of the old winery and give the vintage of the wines that the demijohns once contained.

Château
Prieuré-Lichine
1920

ABOVE Rows of dirty and dusty hand-blown old vases, with lots of irregularities, which make them all the more desirable. Originally used for storing olive oil, pickling vegetables, or preserving fruit, they would now look very attractive filled with flowers and branches.

GLASS BOTTLES AND JARS

Decorative glassware of all types and sizes can make very attractive displays. Large glass jars and bottles, such as demijohns and carboys, are to be found at flea markets the world over. Traditionally, demijohns, which have no branding on them, were used to transport wines to market for sale. Often they would have a wicker casing around the bottom, providing safety and stability. Carboys, on the other hand, tended to be used for transporting acids.

Today, we love these big colorful flagons as decorative interior accessories—they look fantastic in kitchens and informal spaces, especially the bright green and blue ones when gleamingly clean and the sun shines through them, throwing colorful shadows against the walls.

It's important to be mindful of the original contents of a jar or bottle—they may have once graced the shelves of an apothecary or pharmacy. Take particular note of old bottles with slanted shoulders, which were designed to hold poison; their shape was to remind people of a coffin and therefore represent danger! For obvious reasons, carboys should be cleaned before use, but most glass items would benefit from being filled with warm soapy water to remove any residue or staining. If this is not effective, try hydrochloric acid or a limescale-removing agent, but always use with caution and follow the manufacturer's instructions.

You will probably come across a great number of large, thinly blown glass jars, with an attractive green tinge. Originally from Eastern Europe, these hand-blown vessels were used for pickling fruit or cucumbers. Today, they are often filled with flowers.

RIGHT Chunky vintage bottles and a Kilner jar have so much more charm than their modern-day counterparts. Brown and green glass was traditionally used for products, such as beer, that would spoil if exposed to the light.

CULINARY ANTIQUES

COOKING UTENSILS AND EQUIPMENT ARE ALL PART OF OUR SOCIAL HISTORY. CROSSING CONTINENTS ON MY FLEA-MARKET JOURNEY GAVE ME AN INSIGHT INTO HOW PEOPLE IN THE PAST USED TO LIVE, COOK, AND EAT. THE GREATEST PLEASURE TO BE HAD WITH A LOT OF THESE ITEMS IS THAT THEY ARE ALSO BEAUTIFUL DECORATIONS, ADDING A UNIQUE SENSE OF CHARACTER TO THE HOME.

The contents of our modern-day kitchens are very different from those of even just a few decades ago. We tend to use machines and multitasking electrical gadgets to carry out many of the kitchen tasks that were once done by hand. Over time, as these items have become redundant, they have made their way onto flea-market stalls. Some pieces are bought and then displayed as nostalgic decoration, while others may still have a useful purpose in the keen cook's kitchen.

You are likely to come across tables displaying assorted kitchen items, all from one home, as part of a house clearance. Rummaging through and identifying these pieces is one of the greatest pleasures of flea-market trips, often bringing back childhood memories of older relatives using similar ones.

Home refrigeration didn't really become commonplace until the early twentieth century. Until then, food was shopped for on a daily basis, and any items cooked in advance would have been stored in a larder—a cool, airy cupboard built in the kitchen, often fitted out with a stone or marble slab. Small meat safes, also known as pie safes and cool cabinets, were used to keep butter, eggs, and meat for a little longer. Often lined with lead, they were ventilated via a small disc with holes, which allowed the air to circulate, and fitted with a fine mesh, to keep out the flies.

RIGHT A sunny day at Shepton Mallet Antiques Fair in Somerset, England. This wonderful array of kitchen accessories from the 1950s and '60s includes a cream enamel coffee pot, an early cool cabinet, lead-lined for insulation, some china oddments, starched linen dishtowels, and a pretty hand-painted silverware box, all of which could either be used as originally intended or form part of a nostalgic display.

RIGHT This vendor, also at the Shepton Mallet Antiques Fair, specializes in kitchenalia. Everything on sale is in immaculate condition, from old green glass Kilner jars for pickling and preserving, wooden breadboards, plates, and mysterious utensils that give no clue of their original function.

WOOD AND BASKETWARE

So many everyday domestic items from the past have become strong decorative additions to the modern home, but none more so than dough bowls. Round or oblong (known as trenchers), these wooden bowls were used for kneading dough and making batches of loaves for the week ahead. If you intend to use them for food, try to find out how they were used previously—they may have been painted or varnished on the inside—so that you can make them food-safe. They will need to be thoroughly scoured with a nylon scrubber and also conditioned to preserve them—a mineral oil works best. They make attractive table centers in modern interiors, filled with anything from dried flowers to vegetables and fruit.

Rustic basketware also lends a nostalgic air to the home, and can be used practically, often as originally intended, or purely decoratively.

LEFT The Belgian vendor at this stall at Round Top Antiques Fair, Texas, has made a really attractive display out of old wooden bowls from France and Belgium. Hand-carved and dating from around 1850, they were originally used for kneading dough, at a time when bread was home-baked in large batches for the week ahead. The vintage child's bicycle is a good example of the quirky combination of artifacts often found on flea-market stalls.

BELOW An attractive display of basketware covers a wall at Big Daddy's Antiques in San Francisco. A similar approach would work well in a domestic kitchen. The baskets, all made from rattan, were originally used for laundry in the French country houses in the early 1900s, and had somehow found their way to California!

SILVERWARE AND FLATWARE

Identifying silver and its hallmarks is not that difficult if you know what you are looking for. There will almost always be a manufacturer's mark on the underside of a piece—which there will not be for silver plate—and these you can identify from a number of websites, simply by searching for "silver and sterling silver marks." Listings are given by country. Very early silverware, from 1784 to 1890, will have the image of the current sovereign's head, indicating that the appropriate tax or duty would have been paid. A lion's head or lion passant clarifies the silver quality.

A simple way to clean silverware, as well as silver plate, is to line a bucket with aluminum foil, shiny side up. Fill the bucket with warm water and sprinkle in some sodium bicarbonate. Immerse the silver and leave for approximately 30 minutes, then place on a towel and wipe dry with a soft cloth. This method works particularly well on silver plate, as no rubbing is required, which would remove some of the silver plate. Alternatively, use a silver cleaning cloth from a hardware store. Sterling silver can also be washed in the dishwasher on a short cycle, but don't do this for silver plate.

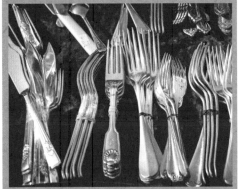

TOP A selection of knives, bundled up and sold by the dozen or half-dozen, with handles of either bone, ivory, or Bakelite.

ABOVE A mixture of silver and silver-plate knives and forks. I have a big selection of similar pieces at home, which I use every day. The silver pieces even go in the dishwasher!

ABOVE Silver-service trays are rarely used now, but back in the days of grand houses and formal dinners, they were commonplace. A handsome silver tray can be used for far more than serving food or drink—it can look charming on a dressing table as a reflective surface to show off perfume bottles, under a vase of flowers, or mounted on the wall as a piece of decorative art.

LEFT Soup spoons, serving spoons, and dessert spoons, some of which appear to be early Georgian silver, can fetch a hefty sum. Silver plate from around the same period, manufactured in Sheffield, England, is a lot cheaper and can be found in abundance at flea markets all over the world.

ENAMELWARE

From a practical as well as an aesthetic point of view, old enamelware has always been hard to resist. The instantly recognizable Falcon white enamel, with a dark blue rim, has a very nostalgic feel. First manufactured in England in 1920, it is often on sale at flea markets. Then there is the enamelware produced in Poland in the 1960s with its gorgeous retro colors.

Enamel cookware was first produced in Germany in 1760. Cast-iron pots were coated with enamel on the inside as a way of preventing food from taking on the taste of the metal as it cooked. Enamelware soon caught on throughout Europe and arrived in the U.S. in the early 1800s. In the mid-nineteenth century, there was a real thrust of creativity as mottled, marbled, and brightly colored enamelware was introduced to the marketplace.

Don't be put off buying stained enamelware—it can be cleaned relatively simply. Start with a bowl of warm water, a sponge, and some light detergent, to remove the obvious grime. If you feel that something more abrasive is needed, use baking soda on the soft side of a cleaning sponge and rub gently. If that doesn't do the trick, make a paste from lemon juice and baking soda, spread evenly over the enamel, and leave for 30 minutes. Then agitate with the rough side of a cleaning sponge, rinse, and wipe with a towel.

TOP Lightweight, easy to clean, and cheap, vintage enamelware, whether in the original white or the later bright colors, has always been popular. Avoid buying chipped enamel if you intend using it for cooking because it may rust.

ABOVE It's quite possible that these enamel wash bowls came from an old hospital. There is a story that, in London during World War II, it was the job of junior staff to hold these bowls over patients' heads as protection whenever an air-raid siren went off.

RIGHT Although it is slightly marked and chipped on the handle, this is a good example of an early twentieth-century enamel casserole pot. A simple way to tell the age of enamelware is to give it a sharp tap on the bottom. If it sounds hollow, it is an early example. Later pieces sound tinny. Unmarked inside, this casserole pot could still be used for cooking.

BELOW The holes in the lids of these vintage enamel food containers allowed the steam to escape during cooking. A new practical use for them would be as a container for waste food destined for the compost heap. Otherwise, they would make very attractive display accents, especially in a country kitchen.

KITCHEN PARAPHERNALIA

Hunting for antique kitchen equipment and utensils is a fascinating journey of discovery. The pieces are not always easy to identify, especially if they are no longer relevant in today's kitchen, having been replaced by snazzy appliances, or the task is no longer performed at home. However, there are some pieces that are timeless, such as coffee grinders and scissors that have the same function today as they always have.

The only reason to replace scissors is if they are rusty or blunt. Not surprisingly, these are the type you will come across most often at flea markets, but don't let that put you off. If rust is preventing scissors from opening, spray a lubricant like WD-40 on the joints. To remove the rust, add half a cup of salt to a bowl and pour in enough warm water to form a thick paste. Spread this evenly over a piece of brown paper and cut through the paper with your scissors—you will see the blades become clean with each cut. Rub over the scissors with half a lemon, rinse the scissors well, and dry with a cloth. To sharpen the blades, cut through thick pieces of steel wool.

ABOVE These old wooden coffee grinders, jumbled together in two metal milk crates, could still be used for their original purpose. Although known more for its cars, Peugeot made the first moulins à café out of wood in 1840, and these were considered the best quality out there.

ABOVE This large mesh frame is an eyecatching way to display vintage scissors of all types and sizes. The very first scissors were made in Egypt in around 1580 BC—we have been snipping for a long time!—and they are surely one of the most practical things in the kitchen drawer today. Never leave scissors wet, as this will hasten the rusting process.

ABOVE It was particularly fashionable in the 1970s to have matching utensils in bright colors that coordinated with the whole kitchen scheme. Represented in this matching set of blue enamelware is a Bundt pan, or ring mold, used for making cakes. As it is in very good condition, it could probably still be used, unlike the graters, which have rusted.

Most flea-market shoppers looking for culinary antiques are after decorative objects to give their kitchens some character, whether to liven up a wall or simply to sit on a shelf. Nothing does that better than copper kettles and jelly molds, which can be made to gleam. They will also last for ever—literally. The very early copper pieces were hand-rolled and will probably now have their fair share of dents. Thicker copper and a heavier weight indicate veteran pieces.

Copper jelly molds displayed on the wall look stunning. Show off their good looks by washing them in warm, soapy water, then rinsing and gently polishing them as you dry, to give a nice shine. You could also try a squirt of ketchup on a cloth to rub off any stains. There are commercial copper cleaning cloths available that can be used periodically to retain the shine.

Old copper containers can also be used for cooking, provided they are thoroughly cleaned beforehand. Always check that the lining is completely intact and sealed, otherwise the taste of the metal can seep into your food. Avoid using hard metal utensils, as they will scratch the surface.

ABOVE These are wonderful examples of pots and molds on sale at Ardingly Antiques & Collectors Fair in Sussex, England. Copper cookware conducts heat quickly and has been popular with professional chefs and cooks since the 1800s. However, there is evidence that copper cooking vessels have existed since 9000 BC. For a long time now, tin has been used as the liner because copper is considered bad for the health.

RIGHT Old bread pans often have the name of the baker stamped on the bottom. These bread pans are unusual in that they have stenciled letters on one end, another way, perhaps, of identifying the contents.

ABOVE The obvious drawback of these three French kitchen canisters is that their lids are missing. However, it could still be worth buying them, if the price were very good, because you could probably eventually find lids that fit. Rummaging through other stands at other flea markets on a specific quest is half the fun of this type of shopping!

LEFT Denby pottery was started in 1809 and is still going strong. This selection of stone stew pots is from the 1970s, seen here at Ardingly Antiques Fair in Sussex, England.

STORAGE JARS

By far my favorite storage jars are the French enamel ones that always seem to be on sale at flea markets, but it's surprising how expensive they can be—whole sets in immaculate condition fetch large sums of money. Interestingly, you would expect them to be cheaper in France than in the U.S. and elsewhere in Europe, but this isn't generally the case. As with all vintage and flea-market finds, a lot depends on their condition. If you want to use them in your kitchen, it's important for the inside to be intact and food-safe. (See tips for cleaning enamelware on page 100.)

Glass as storage takes on a number of different guises—bottles, jars, flagons, the list is endless—but small vintage glass jars that were once filled with preserves and jams are the most fashionable. There are many fine examples on the market, although some are reproductions—check with the vendor—and you can usually get them at a fair price. They are especially popular for parties and weddings, used as centerpieces filled with bunches of meadow flowers or as holders for tea lights.

Made from heavy faceted glass, they predate jars with screw tops. They would have been sealed using paraffin wax, then covered with a pretty cloth, so that the confiture or fruits would be sealed and stored safely. You can, of course, use the jars yourself for the same purpose. Paraffin wax, or baker's wax as it's commonly known, is still available to buy.

In our busy lives, the obvious benefit to buying old glass storage jars is that, apart from particularly fragile pieces, they are safe to put in the dishwasher and can be cleaned and fully restored to be used for all sorts of things, including to store food.

BELOW Early French preserve jars, from before the days of screw lids, can be identified by their soft, round edges. The jars would originally have been sealed with paraffin wax.

BOTTOM All slightly different but all very attractive, this group of vintage preserve jars would look gorgeous en masse, filled with flickering tea lights. The ridges in the glass will cast a reflective glow.

CHAPTER 5:
OBJETS D'ART

COLLECTING THE UNUSUAL

"OBJETS D'ART" LITERALLY MEANS "ART OBJECTS." IT'S AN ALL-ENCOMPASSING TERM FOR ALL THE WONDERFUL THINGS THAT DON'T FIT INTO A SPECIAL CATEGORY—THE QUIRKY, UNUSUAL, INTERESTING, INTRIGUING. THEY'RE NOT NECESSARILY EXPENSIVE BUT THEY ARE ALWAYS BEAUTIFUL IN THE EYE OF THE BEHOLDER. I HAVE A FEW PRECIOUS OBJETS D'ART COLLECTED FROM MARKETS OVER TIME, AND I CHERISH THEM THE MOST.

SCULPTURE

Dating back to prehistoric times, sculpture is one of the oldest forms of art. It is basically the carving or chiseling of a three-dimensional object out of stone, marble, alabaster, or wood. The Ancient Eyptians used sculpture in their temples and gardens to depict their gods. Later, the Ancient Greeks and Romans also surrounded themselves with their gods. The classical style of sculpture reappeared in the Renaissance and remained popular until the end of the nineteenth century.

Stone statues are used mostly in the garden because they are heavy and hardwearing, lasting for many years. However, large statues that have been kept in the garden and have weathered accordingly will look stunning in a modern home, blurring the lines between inside and out.

BELOW This early twentieth-century stone statue of a small child would originally have been used as a garden ornament. The obvious signs of weathering and aging both add to its charm and desirability.

OPPOSITE The mustache and hairstyle on this bust indicate that it was probably sculpted in the nineteenth century, when mustaches were the fashion among men, particularly the aristocracy. The statue has obviously spent a lot of time outdoors, as it is covered in bird excrement and grime. Don't let something like that put you off buying a piece that in every other way is perfect —a gentle clean will probably remove the worst of it. The red "sold" dot, like a bindi, is a sign that someone thought it was worth the price.

Marble is a type of limestone. It occurs in a large range of colors and variegations, and the different types are named after the quarry from which they are taken—probably the most famous is Carrara in Italy. Unlike alabaster, marble can be highly polished, making it more attractive for indoor decorative sculptures. It also has a visual depth, evoking a certain realism.

Often white and translucent, alabaster is not so heavy or hardwearing as marble or stone but it is cheaper. At markets, you will often find smaller decorative pieces made of alabaster, such as lamp bases and figurines.

Wooden sculptures will always be found in markets but their condition will vary enormously according to the age of the piece and how they have been been stored. Plaster of Paris was mainly used for making casts and molds but also to simulate the appearance of wood, stone, or metal.

If a sculpture is chipped or showing signs of deterioration, cleaning it may cause further damage, so be as gentle as you can. For stone, alabaster, marble, and plaster of Paris, begin with a bucket of warm water and scrub with a brush, working slowly but firmly until the grime has gone. For wood, rub it gently first with coarse wire wool, then a finer grade.

BELOW A mid-century rosewood sideboard boasts an arresting collection of objets d'art: the statue of the child is probably made of alabaster because marble tends to be darker; with its art-deco styling, the bronze deer and child on a marble base is from the 1930s; a group of lions on a base, either stone or artificial stone, made in a mold; a large terracotta head of a man on a marble stand; a walnut mantel clock from the 1700s, when Roman numerals were more common on clock faces (always check a clock is in working order before you buy, unless you are happy to have one that is purely decorative).

RIGHT Found at the flea market in Montpellier, southern France, this white alabaster reclining child on a basin is from the 1700s and most likely Italian simply because the vendor was Italian. The French markets, especially those closer to Italy, have many Italian traders selling a good range of marble and alabaster statues.

ABOVE This diverse selection of molded wall plaques features, from top left to right: molded floral and decorative motifs, with the round, green plaque made of plaster of Paris and painted to look like verdigris; the command to "grow" on a piece of beveled wood would make a humorous form of decoration on a wall in a yard; an attractive wooden owl, rustling its wings, probably came originally from an emblem for a business or school; sitting on a plinth is a stone bust of a Greek god, the surface bubbles suggesting that it was made in a mold using plaster of Paris.

RIGHT The fine details in this statue of a mother and child would make a stunning piece in the hallway of a large formal home. It is an imposing piece made of either marble or alabaster, and its size and quality indicate that was probably a special commission.

BELOW A rather sinister collection of vintage African masks. It is worth getting as much information as possible about such pieces from the seller because the history is of such enormous cultural interest. It is likely that these are up to 75 years old—masks older than that are hard to find. Trust the seller, who should know their stock and will have attached a price tag accordingly. You can identify particular tribes by searching the many sites online.

RELIGIOUS ICONS

"Icon" means image. The word usually refers to an image with a religious (often Christian) connotation, meaning, and use. There are many religious icons from all eras to be found at flea markets, and they have become increasingly popular used as decorative pieces. They are prized simply for their beauty.

I find it interesting that all the colors in a religious icon have special significance. In the Christian faith, gold is reserved for Christ and symbolizes divinity. Traditionally, religious icons are gilded in gold leaf. Meanwhile, white is used for heavenly purity, purple is the byzantine symbol of royalty, and red represents blood and symbolizes life on Earth. Blue represents the heavens and the kingdom of God, and green the living earth, used to depict, youth, hope, and the beginning of life. Black, on the other hand, symbolizes evil and death, but not always—many religious orders wear black vestments.

Religious icons come in both two-dimensional pieces, for example, paintings and tiles, and three-dimensional, such as sculptures, molded or cast figures, and wooden carvings. They can span many religions, such as Buddhism, Hinduism, and Catholicism. The three-dimensional figures often add an ethereal feeling of peace and calm to a room, and are wonderful visual reminders of faith and beauty, whether used singly or as a group. They come in marble, stone, and, quite often, wood. Most are purely decorative, although some have a specific purpose, such as candlesticks.

ABOVE These large candlesticks, depicting the Angel Gabriel in his blue robes, would have once adorned a church. Placing them in the home is likely to take some thought, and they would perhaps be more immediately suited to a bar or restaurant, where they could be painted to become part of a rather interesting themed interior.

RIGHT This vintage statuette of a priest has seen better days, and it would be difficult and costly to repair. However, as the piece is unique and would make an eye-catching interior design statement, it is likely to be worth it.

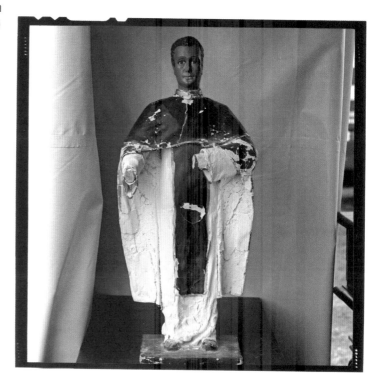

The Christian cross, or crucifix, is often three-dimensional. Nowadays it has great ornamental value in addition to its religious significance. Collecting crosses and crucifixes has become a very popular and rewarding pastime. They are found in so many materials and styles and are particularly striking when grouped together, as shown overleaf.

ABOVE This very beautiful plaster cast of the Virgin Mary was seen on a stand at the Round Top Antiques Fair, Texas. The seller, who specialized in religious icons, displayed pieces with a particular panache. The carved and bronze crucifixes all date from the mid-eighteenth century to the early nineteenth century.

ABOVE At Round Top, Texas, a torso mannequin displays decorative crucifix necklaces. Newly made, they suggest a decorative value, rather than religious.

RIGHT The impact of a wall covered in crucifixes is immense. These are from a number of different countries, in different styles, shapes, and materials, but all representing the same thing, that, according to Christians, Jesus died on the cross to save mankind. The meaning of the crucifix is therefore profound and I think that, regardless of faith, it should not be treated lightly.

TAXIDERMY

The word "taxidermy" has its roots in Greek, meaning the arrangement of skin. It's the art of preparing, stuffing, and mounting the skins, sometimes including the fur, feathers, or scales, of animals for display. The technique can be applied to all vertebrates.

The earliest methods of taxidermy were published back in 1748 in France, although there were several pioneers of the profession throughout Europe. In the nineteenth century, hunters began to bring their trophies to upholstery stores, where the animal skins would be sewn up and stuffed with rags and cotton. The term "stuffed animal" evolved from this crude form of the practice.

The golden age of taxidermy was the Victorian era, when it evolved into an art and stuffed animals appeared anatomically correct. A display of stuffed birds at the Great Exhibition in London in 1851, by the ornithologist John Hancock, sparked enormous interest, and stuffed animals of all descriptions, from hunting trophies to dearly loved pets, soon became fashionable decoration in middle-class homes.

BELOW Vintage green shutters provide an attractive backdrop to an impressive selection of taxidermy, from the real thing to a white reproduction ornamental head. Displaying a stag's head at home is not for everyone—some people find it quite offensive. But if you have no such qualms, it's best to consider only those in good condition, with no holes or marks, as getting them repaired can be a costly business. Rather incongruously, a fairground wizard sits alongside all those antlers.

ABOVE This stuffed lioness, found at Round Top, would have come from a house clearance but, unless the rooms were particularly spacious, I can't think how it would fit into a domestic setting. I can, though, see it forming a dramatic display in a club or bar.

RIGHT This table shows a mixed display of shed antlers and those from dead animals, where a small section of the skull is still attached, fixed to a piece of wood for hanging on the wall. These are increasingly popular in modern interiors.

ABOVE Once fashionable with the Victorians, stuffed deer heads—even rather pretty, doe-eyed ones like this—have become a modern interior design trend.

RIGHT This somewhat surreal photograph shows complete skulls. Before parting with cash for such items, be aware that in order for them to be displayed, they would need to be given mounts, which may bump the overall cost up too much.

ABOVE The large painted iron planter and the two stuffed geese in flight are from the same period and probably from the same house. Their backdrop at the market—a splendid carved mantel surround—creates just the right setting.

Stuffed creatures, a large number of them Victorian, are a feature in many contemporary interiors—I have watched the trend gain momentum over the last ten years. Stags' heads are particularly popular, with the antlers being given different roles, from coat hooks to jewelry stands. Antlers that have been shed naturally also make attractive interior design statements— I have seen them sprayed white or gold, piled into a large bowl, and used as a table centerpiece.

The more pristine a stuffed animal or head, the better and the less likely for any expensive repairs to be needed later on. Keep the pieces out of the sunlight and away from damp, as this will cause mold. Brush the coat or fur regularly with a stiff brush. Stuffed animals should not be kept outdoors, regardless of how tempting it might be! It is possible to clean small deer skulls with antlers by boiling them in a pan of water to remove any dirt or marks, provided they aren't attached to a wooden mount.

OPPOSITE These old suitcases, painted and stenciled, could have a useful second life as storage or bedside tables.

RIGHT Looks can be deceiving. Even if luggage looks only slightly battered on the outside, always get the seller to show you the insides as well. Inspect everything carefully, including the hinges and clasps to make sure it closes properly. Be clear about what you want the luggage for, then decide whether it is fit for purpose.

VINTAGE LUGGAGE

The first thing to do when buying vintage luggage is to check the material. Leather will need careful cleaning with a leather cream or wax and a soft cloth. Soapy water and a sponge will be perfectly fine for vinyl. Cases or trunks made from compressed fiber or wood can be lightly rubbed with a good-quality natural wax and fine-wire wool, to remove any dirt, and then buffed with a soft cloth to restore them to their original color and finish. Wooden chests that have seen a lot of use will need to be rubbed first with coarse wire wool, followed by a finer grade, to remove any grime.

To keep luggage in good condition, avoid placing it in direct sunlight or next to a heat source, such as an open fire or a radiator. Neglected wood or leather could easily crack or split—use a good-quality natural wax from time to time to keep it looking good.

Old luggage often has an odor, generally as a result of years of neglect. One solution is to fill it with charcoal or cat litter, both of which will absorb the smell. Another method is to spray the inside with equal parts of vinegar and water, or give it a sprinkling of bicarbonate of soda. It's important that none of these materials touches leather, as they can cause discoloration.

Much of the vintage luggage on sale at flea markets wouldn't survive if they were to be used as originally intended. However, they have great alternative uses in the home, either as storage, bedside tables, or coffee tables—the size of trunks makes them especially good for this.

ABOVE We are used to luggage being lighter today and, of course, fitted with wheels, so beware of buying a vintage suitcase for traveling because it would probably be too heavy and cumbersome. Used at home, however, as a table or prop, their weight doesn't matter. Stacked high, these suitcases in unusual colors as well as good condition would make very attractive alternative storage.

ABOVE Tailor's dummies or mannequins come in sections, which can be adjusted by turning a button to change the size so that it's right for the garment being modeled.

RIGHT A table of wooden hat blocks, used originally to shape the hat materials and create the various sizes. It's unlikely that anyone would buy a hat block for its original purpose, but it is a great way to display a hat at home and help it keep its shape.

MANNEQUINS

Vintage tailor's dummies, hat molds, glove molds— all vestiges of the clothing industry—make frequent appearances at flea markets. Their history goes back a long way. Wooden mannequins, variously known as dress forms or dummies, originated in the fifteenth century, when they were used to demonstrate clothes for customers and show how an item fitted or looked. Mannequins are still used by tailors and window dressers today. The word comes from the French, meaning an artist's jointed model.

The first papier-mâché mannequins were made in France in the mid-nineteenth century. The most famous manufacturer was a company called Siegel & Stockman, which is still thriving. I have a vivid memory of their mannequins from when I was growing up, so seeing them in such good condition at flea markets is thrilling.

There's no reason why a vintage dummy should not be used in its original role, provided it is in good condition, and although they fetch a high price at flea markets, they would still be cheaper than buying new. But if sewing is not your thing, they make an attractive addition to a bedroom to pin your jewellery on or as practical storage solutions, perhaps for the outfit you plan to wear the next day or for draping over strings of beads or belts. If the mannequin has a head, it becomes the obvious place to keep a few hats.

BELOW A rather ramshackle extended family of display dummies at Round Top, with some even missing their heads! A single dummy would make a fun and practical addition to a bedroom, draped with clothes, while a number of them would brighten up a party, festooned with fairy lights.

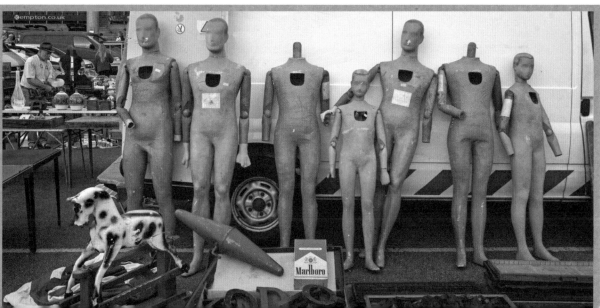

ABOVE I have to admit, when I saw this tableau of purple ribbons with badges of women's faces, I had no idea what they were, but coming across the unexpected is one of the greatest pleasures of treasure hunting. Subsequent research led to me to a fascinating discovery. The ribbons were worn by members of the Degree of Pocahontas at their annual gatherings, called Great Sun Sessions.

This influential group of women was founded in 1885, taking their name from the celebrated character in Native American history, and is heavily involved in philanthropic work. The rich purple color of these ribbons and the badges of smiling faces, so obviously from a bygone era, would create an intriguing display in a glass-fronted memory box and hung on the wall.

RIBBONS AND BANNERS

Ribbons are among the oldest decorative textiles. Used over centuries to adorn clothing, they were a way of changing the look and feel of an outfit, costume, or dress without a huge financial outlay.

I love collecting vintage ribbons. Quite often you will come across a dealer with rolls and rolls of ribbon acquired from old textile manufacturing companies, such as lingerie ribbons in the palest pink grosgrain or satin—luxury ribbons that are no longer readily available. A birthday gift wrapped in vintage ribbon looks incredibly special. Ribbons from before World War II are the most desirable and collectible because, after the war, they started to be made from more synthetic and paper fibers.

Woven banners and advertising strips made from printed fabrics became popular during the 1950s and '60s, when they were widely used in political rallies and sports events. Colorful and decorative, they would make eye-catching wall art, especially in a teenage boy's bedroom. They seem to be unique to the U.S.—I have never come across them in European markets.

BELOW Pegged on a line like washing are a number of banners and initials. The big fabric initials in loop stitch denote fraternity houses, colleges, and sports teams, and would have been sewn onto varsity jackets. They would make striking wall art, as would the highly collectible vintage election campaign banners, especially if they were framed.

BOOKS AND PAPER

Books are collected for reasons other than for reading. They are often bought at flea markets purely for the color of their spines. Arranged by color on bookshelves, they perform almost the same role as wallpaper. I've noticed that hardback books are becoming scarcer at markets, but a house or library clearance will produce a wealth of them all at one time and you may be lucky. In among them, you may find a first edition in very good condition, but you can be confident that the vendor would have noticed this before you and fixed the price accordingly.

Old technical and architectural drawings all make interesting art for walls, as do vintage Ordnance Survey maps in the U.K. and their American equivalent, U.S. Geological Survey (USGS) maps, with their glimpses of towns and villages as they were in the past. I once bought a batch of old maps and wrapped up all my Christmas gifts in them, carefully matching towns or cities to the recipients.

ABOVE This stack of books at the Avignon Antiques Fair in southeastern France represents just a fraction of the work by Voltaire, a prolific eighteenth-century French writer. Their paper covers mean they are more fragile than hardbacks. They will need to be kept dry to prevent mold forming, and out of the sun to stop fading. Regular dusting will also help them last.

RIGHT Knowing that these hardback books will be bought purely for decoration purposes, the vendor has helpfully color-coded them and bound them together with string.

VINTAGE TOYS

TOYS ARE VERY COLLECTIBLE, MAINLY BECAUSE OF THE SENSE OF NOSTALGIA THAT THEY BRING, REMINDING SO MANY OF US OF OUR CHILDHOOD AND AN AGE OF INNOCENCE. PLAYTIME HAS GIVEN WAY TO ELECTRICAL AND DIGITAL GADGETS, AND THE SIMPLE PLEASURE THAT CHILDREN USED TO GET FROM PLAYING WITH A TIN TRUCK OR A WOODEN TOP HAS GONE FOREVER.

The very first toys are almost prehistoric—toys representing animals, for example, have been unearthed at archaeological sites—not that you are likely to come across any that old! More likely are tin toys and teddy bears.

Tin toys date from the 1800s, when they were made from steel covered in tin, which was usually bent and nailed on. It is hard to believe that they were then considered safe for small children. They certainly wouldn't be now and shouldn't be used as toys, especially as they may be covered in lead paint.

Perhaps the most popular toy ever is the teddy bear, and vintage ones are highly collectible. Their design hasn't changed much since the original bears, named after Theodore "Teddy" Roosevelt, were made by Morris Michtom in the U.S. and Steiff in Germany. Steiff bears are easy to recognize because they have a very distinctive, brand label: a red button in the ear.

You may find educational toys, such as jigsaw puzzles, books, and picture or letter identification cards, going back to the nineteenth century. It is fascinating to compare them with their equivalents produced today.

Every trip to a flea market is different from the last, and you never know what you will find at any one of them. I've lost count of the number of times I've said that after a shopping expedition! The photograph overleaf, taken of one stall at Round Top, Texas, illustrates my point perfectly. A U.S. issue rocket is suspended from the roof, with a fine-looking "teddy" in a cowboy outfit sitting astride it. I loved how the vendor had displayed two such polar opposites together, and it made me laugh, but it also made me stop and think about why anyone might want a decommissioned rocket shell in their home! I suppose it's a question of horses for courses, and the same question can be asked about any passionate collector.

ABOVE Wooden toy boats with cloth sails had their heyday in Victorian times, played with by little boys and girls on ponds and lakes. They might even be usable today with a little patching up to make them unsinkable.

OPPOSITE A rather incongruous lamp, fashioned from one-part vintage standard lamp and one-part vintage "Tonka" toy—a pale green pickup truck. The appeal for such a piece could not be wide, but someone out there is sure to love it.

LEFT This is one of the most bizarre displays I came across at Round Top, Texas, proving that often the most unlikely bedfellows make the best decoration. Partnered with a vintage teddy bear, the decommissioned U.S. army rocket shell raises a smile. The backdrop is equally beguiling and raises the question of why the vendor also has for sale a giant letter "M" and "S" and a handsome section of an early eighteenth-century mantel.

BELOW Equally quirky is this giant-sized vintage fiberglass man's head. Originally there would have been a body to accompany the head, and these larger-than-life figures were often used as a form of roadside advertising for diners or gas stations during the 1950s.

CHAPTER 6:
TEXTILES & RUGS

RUGS

THERE ARE SO MANY DIFFERENT STYLES OF RUGS FROM ALL OVER THE WORLD, IN AS MANY FABRICS AND WEAVES, THAT IT'S IMPOSSIBLE TO CATALOG ALL THE OPTIONS HERE. HOWEVER, AS WITH ALL MY VINTAGE BUYING TIPS, IF WHAT YOU SEE IS THE RIGHT COLOR AND THE RIGHT SIZE, AND YOU CONSIDER THE PRICE TAG TO BE FAIR, THEN BUY IT.

The oldest-known rugs date back to Neolithic times. Although I'm not suggesting you will find one that old on your flea-market travels, you will discover rugs of enormous diversity, in size, age, and appearance.

Antique rugs were generally crafted in cotton, silk, and wool. The highest percentage of any material would be wool, which gives the rug its durability, with cotton or silk woven into it. The greater the silk content, the more elegant a rug will appear, and prices will invariably be higher. Handmade Persian rugs—probably the most famous type of rug—have a lot of silk in them, and these still hold their value and also wear very well. Authentic examples are still made in Iran (formerly Persia) by skilled artisans.

The designs of Persian rugs have remained pretty much the same over the years, having been passed down the generations. The weavers use symbols that represent the region where the rug is made, and the layout will be one of four different types: all-over, central medallion, compartment, and one-sided. The knots used in Persian rugs will also help you to authenticate them. Traditionally, they are made with a single looping knot, although more recent examples may include a double looping knot. If this sounds far too complicated, do your research beforehand. Check online, and also be prepared to ask the vendor probing questions—he or she has a reputation to protect, so should not try to pull the wool over your eyes! There are,

RIGHT Hanging over a railing, as well as covering the grass, is a selection of antique and reproduction kilim and Persian rugs, also at Ardingly. Trust plays a great part in flea-market shopping when you are starting out. Always quiz the vendor about the age and history of their stock, as well as putting faith in your instincts. Check carefully for marks and stains too.

RIGHT On display at Ardingly Antiques & Collectors Fair in Sussex, England, is a pale-colored Turkish kilim alongside a diamond design rug with tassels. The geometric design suggests that it has been made by the Beni Ourain from Morocco, but an original would be very expensive and certainly too precious to be displayed hanging on a fence at a country fair.

however, many fake "Persian" rugs on the market. These are usually machine-made using mercerized cotton or synthetic fibers. Check a rug's label for the country of origin; if it is not made in Iran, it is not Persian, but an oriental rug.

Turkish rugs also have a long history, going back to Neolithic times. The flatweave variety, kilims, have a much more casual appearance than pile rugs and for that reason are particularly popular now in Western homes. As with Persian rugs, their patterns have been passed down the generations. Genuine Turkish rugs will always use natural dyes, which means they will fade in direct sunlight. However, I love their faded colors—for me they give a real air of authenticity and history, which makes them very collectible.

A handmade rug—almost always made from wool and silk—will always command a higher price than a machine-made one. To check if a rug is handmade or not, take a look at the underside. If the pattern is visible, this usually means it is handmade. Machine-made rugs have a thick backing and you won't be able to see the pattern. With a handmade rug, you should also be able to see the knots on the underside.

Buying a rug with a stain is a risky business unless, of course, it's inconspicuous or you don't mind it being there. The stain is likely to have set and have been in place a long time. That means it will be very difficult, if not impossible, to remove, as you won't know what caused it. You could take the rug to a restorer but satisfactory results won't be guaranteed and you may end up parting with a hefty amount of money for nothing.

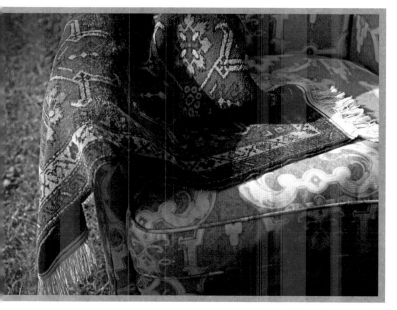

LEFT By doing some preliminary research and knowing what to expect in terms of color and pattern, you can make an educated guess about whether a Persian rug like this is genuine or a reproduction. If the vendor says it's valuable, ask to see the supporting documents.

ABOVE Turkish and Moroccan rugs are a common
sight at French fairs. Seen here at the antique market
in Montpellier, southern France, is a selection of
exotic-looking, rather interesting rugs, weighted down
by mounted animal skulls and horns, and, even more
incongruously, a 1930s molded metal sun lounger.

THROWS AND BLANKETS

I DEFINITELY HAVE A WEAKNESS FOR THROWS AND BLANKETS, WHICH I HAVE COLLECTED THROUGH THE YEARS. MY ENTHUSIASM HAS MEANT THAT I HAVE MORE THAN I NEED AND CERTAINLY MORE THAN I CAN USE AT ANY ONE TIME. FOR THAT REASON, THEY ARE ON ROTATION AT HOME, MOSTLY IN ACCORDANCE WITH THE SEASONS, BUT I ALSO USE THE WASHABLE ONES TO PROTECT MY SOFA FROM DOGGY PAWS.

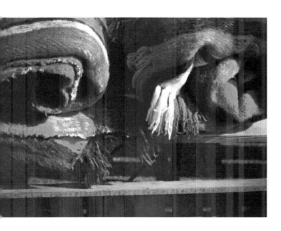

ABOVE A stack of fringed Welsh blankets in rich, burnt orange colors, on sale at Shepton Mallet Antiques Fair in Somerset, England. Always check for moth holes before buying—you may want to take the risk that the moths and their larvae, which make the holes, are long gone—but it's good to know what you might be up against. Pass over any soiled blankets, as it's unlikely that you will ever be able to remove the stains.

OPPOSITE A spectacular selection of vibrantly colored "tapestry" Welsh blankets, in a beautiful array of colors, also seen at Shepton Mallet Antiques Fair.

There is a tradition of giving blankets as wedding presents and of passing them down through the generations. The vintage blankets you are likely to encounter at flea markets will more often than not come with their unique rich history, which adds to their charm.

Welsh blankets are a particular favorite of mine. Usually edged with blanket stitch, they are basically two different pieces of cloth woven together on a dobby loom to form a double cloth. Many distinctive styles have evolved over the years, with plaids and checks being the most common pattern. Then there is the misleadingly named "tapestry" Welsh blanket, which isn't made from tapestry at all but from a double-ply woolen yarn.

These blankets are made across Wales, although production is focused mainly in the north of the country, and has been since the eighteenth century. Most Welsh blankets on sale at flea markets tend to date from the 1950s and 1960s.

Honeycomb or waffle woolen blankets are very distinctive—I find those in pastel colors particularly attractive. The honeycombing makes them slightly spongy to the touch. The double weave, where one color is woven on top of another, gives a shadowy effect.

A drawback of woolen blankets is that they are susceptible to moths. One or two tiny holes in a vintage blanket might not spoil its appearance but you would be wise to have it dry-cleaned when you get home, just in case the larvae are still present. Caring for blankets is much the same as for any woolen item. When not in use, store blankets somewhere dry with mothballs or more pleasantly scented cedar balls. Use sealable containers but remove the blankets periodically to keep them aired.

LEFT Two very different types of woven cloth on display at the Round Top Antiques Fair in Texas. The red-and-white banner, from the turn of the nineteenth century, once hung at meetings of the I.O.O.F., which stands for the Independent Order of Oddfellows, a benevolent society, while FLT represents their motto of Friendship, Love, and Truth. The second piece of cloth is probably a tablecloth, from Sweden, beautifully decorated in huck embroidery, where no stitches are visible on the reverse of the material. This style of embroidery was at the height of popularity during the 1930s and '40s. Older pieces of cloth like these often come with iron mold, which you might be able to remove by applying table salt, lemon juice, or cream of tartar before washing.

BELOW In a glorious array of blues, these floral, gingham, and the original striped seersucker eiderdowns are very tempting. The word "seersucker" comes from the Persian *shir o shakkar*, meaning milk and sugar, a figurative reference to the striped cloth. This puckered, all-cotton fabric is lightweight and perfect for summer bedcovers.

TEXTILES

COMING UPON A STACK OF VINTAGE NATURAL LINEN IN A FRENCH MARKET—THE MOST USUAL PLACE TO FIND THE REAL THING—IS FOR ME INCREDIBLY EXCITING BUT, SADLY, THERE IS NOT SO MUCH OF IT AROUND THESE DAYS. IF I DO SPOT A LINEN STALL, I FIND IT IMPOSSIBLE TO LEAVE WITHOUT PURCHASING SOMETHING— THE HEAVY, NATURAL, SLUBBY TEXTURE OF OLD LINEN IS SO BEAUTIFUL.

ABOVE Vendors will usually oblige and cut up lengths, by the yard or meter, from rolls of vintage linen—generally, the width is about 21in (53cm). The linen will often come with a stripe, with blue or red the most common. Originally, these rolls would probably have been destined for making dishtowels because linen is so absorbent.

LINEN

Linen, made from the flax plant, has wonderful qualities and is used for clothing and soft furnishings. The textile can be traced back to Egypt over 5,000 years ago, where, rather romantically, it was called "woven moonlight." The cultivation of flax made its way west over time and it is still flourishing in Belgium, specifically Flanders, in spite of the increasing popularity around the world of cotton and synthetic fibers as a result of the Industrial Revolution. The production of linen now, though, is a much more eco-friendly process, and hydrogen peroxide is used to bleach the flax, instead of chlorine, which further reduces any negative impact on the environment.

Linen in the home is easy to look after. It is the strongest natural fiber known to man, and examples of it, particularly bed linen, which is often embroidered with a monogram, are passed down the generations as family heirlooms because of its longevity.

The more you wash linen, the softer it becomes, and the wetness during washing actually increases its strength, meaning that it stands up well to rigorous laundering if there are any stains that need to be removed. Owing to its smooth surface, linen loses stains easily, but you will still need to work on them in the same way you would for other fabrics, before placing in the washing machine. Ordinary household soaps and washing powders can be used, but avoid bleaching agents, as these will weaken the fibers. Hang linen out to dry, if you can, and iron while damp. As for all textiles, it is advisable to store linen on slatted shelves to provide air circulation and reduce the risk of moths and mold. Store sheets and pillowcases rolled because, if folded, they will quickly adopt the fold mark.

ABOVE A mixture of linen and hemp rolls seen here at Montpellier Antiques Market in southwestern France. Hemp is a variety of the cannabis plant grown for its fiber, and used industrially to make rope and string. These rolls in the foreground would originally have been made into grain sacks. It has a much rougher, raw quality than linen, so its use in the home is more limited.

LEFT These grain sacks can be cut up and made into cushion covers as well as covers for day beds. Other than soiling and stains, vintage linen is unlikely to be damaged. Some stains may come out through washing but don't depend on it.

LEFT Rolls of striped cotton satin, sold by the meter, on display at the Avignon Antiques Fair in southwestern France. This fabric is relatively hardwearing, lightweight, and washable—perfect for upholstery, curtains, and blinds. I can also see it made up into deep, button-mattress-style bench covers.

OPPOSITE BELOW These neatly displayed linen sacks, originally from Eastern Europe—probably Hungary or Ukraine—are in a herringbone pattern. At least 70 years old, they were made on a handloom but, being so robust, they don't look their age. They are a wonderful piece of history. Linen is fairly easy to work with, and I bought nine of these sacks to cover an armchair at home.

BELOW These rolls of linen and stacks of linen sheets can be used to make various things in the home, such as summer-weight bed covers or top sheets. If you have a project in mind, take careful measurements before you leave home so that you can work out how much you will need to buy—the width of the rolls means that you will probably have to join pieces together. Always check for stains before you buy, and wash them once you get them home.

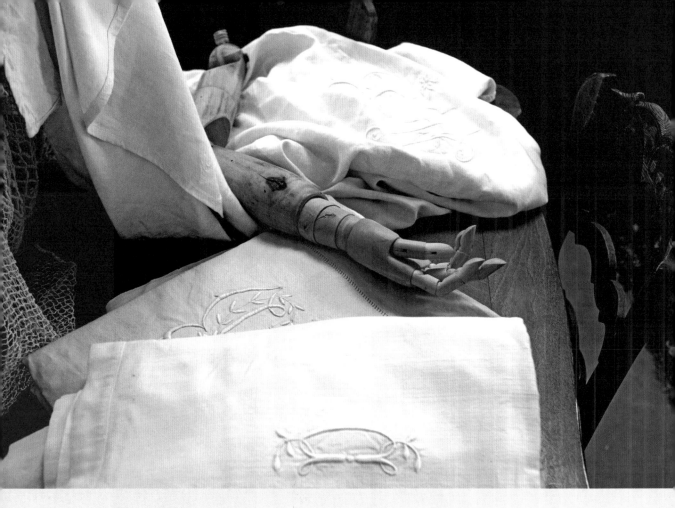

ABOVE Beautiful monogrammed linen sheets, seen here at the Isle-sur-la-Sorgue market in Provence. Monogramming bed linen was traditionally undertaken by girls for their trousseau. The pieces often feature only the girl's initials, as the future husband wouldn't be known at that point. However, giving monogrammed linen as a wedding gift, with the initials of both husband and wife, was a popular tradition. I love searching for bed linen with the initials of people I know—it makes a wonderful gift.

EMBROIDERY

Embroidery is a textile craft that uses needle and thread to decorate fabric. The stitching was traditionally done by hand but, today, it is usually done by machine, which is less labor-intensive and therefore cheaper. However, it will take a keen eye and close scrutiny to tell the difference between authentic hand embroidery and machine embroidery. Mistakes in embroidery and also small differences in design, if you are comparing several items together—individual pieces of hand embroidery in a set are rarely identical—are a sign of handmade origins, and for that you will pay a premium.

Embroidery has a rich cultural heritage the world over, going back to China in around 3500 BC, where it was seen as a symbol of wealth. It has been used to illustrate great events in history—the Bayeux Tapestry, for example, embroidered in the late eleventh century, depicts the Battle of Hastings. Later, in Europe and the U.S., embroidery developed into a respectable pastime for young ladies, and the Great Exhibition in 1851, held in London, and the arrival of women's magazines helped to spread the word.

ABOVE Different types of embroidered cloth, including a Chinese design on satin in vivid green and red, and some machine-embroidered tablecloths and matching place mats. Popular in the 1950s and '60s, these are made of synthetic fibers, probably polyester or rayon, and would have been used for "best" in modern households at the time.

RIGHT On display with a nineteenth-century, lace-edged table runner and tablecloth, the machine-embroidered tablecloths and their matching napkins from the 1960s to '70s are too perfect to have been stitched by hand. Always check embroidery for staining and tears. As pieces like these are quite easy to find at flea markets, it's best to pass over anything that's not in perfect condition.

TABLE LINENS AND PRINTED FABRICS

Buying a tablecloth at a flea market is often rewarding but it can be frustrating——I have bought the wrong size on so many occasions, and have also noticed a stain in exactly the wrong place only when I'm back at home! Make sure you inspect your prospective purchases carefully and you have the measurements of your table at hand. Allow a minimum of a 2-ft (½-meter) drop, unless you want the cloth to touch the ground. Tables are not a uniform width or length, and vintage cloths will not always fit modern tables. Some French tables can be unusually narrow, although my old French country table is unusually wide! Vintage linen sheets make great table covers, which I use when friends join me for dinner. I like to starch my white tablecloths——they look so inviting, especially when accompanied by the twinkle of candles.

There are amazing patterned fabrics to be found at markets, sometimes as original bolts of cloth or as curtains, which you can unpick and turn into something else. Smaller quantities of fabric are great for making into a quilt or cushions and pillows. You will come across a lot of discontinued patterns, so bear in mind that you are unlikely to be able to buy the same pattern again. Also, remember that fabrics on sale at a flea market, in whatever form, will nearly always have been kept in storage, so check for damage caused by damp.

Market vendors who trade in old stock, including yarn, lace, and embroidery, are knowledgeable about their wares. Some old fabrics can be washed without causing any harm, but others may need to be dry-cleaned. If you can find out the fabric brand and pattern from the vendor, you should be able to research the exact composition of the piece for cleaning purposes.

OPPOSITE FAR LEFT This cross section of fabric remnants makes a tempting display, putting all kinds of ideas into your head about what to make with them. Measure the fabric before buying to make sure there is enough for a particular project. It would be very challenging to find more of a remnant fabric if you needed to, although you will sometimes find the name of the brand and pattern printed along the selvage, which would make research easier.

ABOVE These heavily patterned chintz remnants, seen at Kempton Park market, in the south of England, are typical of curtain fabrics that were popular during the 1970s and '80s.

OPPOSITE LEFT At the Round Top Antiques Fair in Texas, I came across this cotton retro State tablecloth from c.1955. These were very popular with tourists at the time, and are now highly collectible.

VINTAGE CLOTHING

MY PREVIOUSLY LIMITED KNOWLEDGE OF BUYING VINTAGE CLOTHING
PROMPTED ME TO DO SOME RESEARCH FOR THIS BOOK BY TALKING
TO VENDORS AT FAIRS AND MARKETS. FROM WHAT I HAVE LEARNED,
I NOW KNOW THERE ARE SOME KEY THINGS TO BE AWARE OF.

If you are a fan of the retro look, then buying vintage clothing is probably already a hobby, but finding garments of your chosen era in good condition, and with no moth holes or stains, can be a formidable task.

Most vintage clothes sellers are dedicated and professional and will have a thorough knowledge of periods and designers throughout the years, so a lot of information can be gained just by talking to them. But you can also find out a lot yourself.

Sewn-in labels can also provide valuable clues, such as whether the piece is a designer brand, which, of course, will affect the price tag. Check for stains, particularly under the armpits—deodorant or sweat stains are very unlikely to come out—as well as for moth holes, tears, or burns, by holding a garment up to the light. This will also show if the fabric has worn thin. Ask yourself if any damage can be repaired. If you know a good dressmaker, you may not be daunted by the need to alter garments, or you may even be a dab hand at stitching yourself. If specialist repair is required, do you love the piece enough to go to all the trouble and expense? If there are fastenings, such as beautiful buttons but one is missing, this will mean changing the entire set, which could prove overall too costly. Dresses or coats that came originally with a self-covered belt but which is now missing will represent a problem unless a plain belt will look the part.

Remember that sizing over the years has changed as women's shapes have altered and filled out, so ignore any size labels. The best thing to do at a market, if you can't try on a piece, is to hold it up against you and check in the mirror.

RIGHT A well-displayed stand at Round Top, where the more valuable hats and accessories are covered with glass domes to protect them. This is a good sign that the vendor cares about his stock and, by extension, his customers. When trying on hats, ask for a mirror and take your time. You must feel confident you have found one that fits and suits the shape of your face, otherwise you might get it home and decide never to wear it. Never buy a hat that has lost its shape. Taking along an honest but diplomatic friend is always a good idea!

BELOW Pegged up at Round Top market is this beautiful selection of vintage leather gloves, in the palest pink. Always try on gloves for size, and check for marks and stains. Cleaning leather gloves requires a leather wash.

ABOVE Another tempting display at Round Top, this time of a rail of retro dresses in small floral prints from the 1940s, '50s, and '60s. To achieve the right figure for them and not look frumpy, you will need a three-quarter-length petticoat to lift the skirt, and a bullet bra—a padded conical bra invented in the late 1940s—to give you the necessary curves.

RIGHT This selection of fine lace and satin lingerie is for a more demure look. The lace is particularly fragile, and such items require careful handling. Hand-wash only in warm water with soap flakes or a special lingerie wash.

Check the soles of footwear for wear and holes—it's useful to know that modern methods of shoe repair may not be suitable for delicate vintage shoes. Also, make sure the leather is not cracked, which would be uncomfortable, and that there are no missing buckles or buttons, which would be almost impossible to replace.

Dresses with nipped-in waists, where the emphasis is on the bust, will benefit from a proper retro bra, like a bullet bra. These will give the body the correct shape for the look you are after, and also help with posture. Always check the elastic—if there is no stretch, don't buy it. A girdle from the same era will also improve appearances, but if it makes a cracking sound when stretched, again, don't buy it, as this means it is breaking apart. A petticoat can make a big difference to the silhouette of a full-skirted garment—dresses from the 1950s and '60s will require a mid-calf, net petticoat.

Another consideration when buying vintage lingerie is gauging whether it will fit or not, particularly as body shapes have changed over the years. There are usually no changing rooms at flea markets, so, if the vendor is willing, you may have to improvise and try things on in the restrooms.

BELOW These shapeless and heavy linen nightshirts for men and women, some of them with embroidered monograms, would have been usual attire during the nineteenth century. As well as not being very comfortable to wear against the skin, they are not really practical in today's centrally heated homes. I think they are probably best cut up and turned into covers for cushions and pillows.

CHAPTER 7:
FOR THE GARDEN

TABLES AND CHAIRS

THERE IS ALWAYS A LOT OF GARDEN FURNITURE AT MARKETS, BUT IT IS SEASONAL AND YOU WILL FIND THE BEST SELECTION DURING THE SUMMER. SOME OF MY FAVORITE THINGS ARE THE GARDEN FURNITURE PURCHASES I HAVE MADE OVER THE YEARS. HOWEVER, I HAVE BROUGHT MANY OF THE PIECES INDOORS, WHERE THEY NOW LIVE COMFORTABLY ALONGSIDE UPHOLSTERED FURNITURE.

When buying tables and chairs, keep a checklist of things to consider: do they need to be weatherproof; what is the size of the space you have allocated for them; what style will best suit your yard; and how many people will you need to seat at any one time?

Much of the outdoor furniture on sale at markets will be as the result of a house clearance—it's the same for indoor furniture. Its condition will be very varied, depending primarily on how long it has stood outside bearing the ravages of time. Some wear and tear is very desirable—rust, mildew, and moss are most attractive and add to the charm—but there is a point when these elements are excessive and even close to destroying a piece. In such cases, consider carefully whether restoration is desirable and affordable.

French café tables, made of wrought iron, from the 1930s have become very popular. They often have a hole in the middle, where a parasol would have been placed, but the ones without a hole are the rarest. I'm lucky enough to have one, and it is in my living room with a table lamp on top. Any original paint on tables of this age will now be very worn, if not completely peeling off, leaving the metal exposed and causing rust. Sanding them down and then treating with a powder coating—a type of paint that covers with an epoxy resin and gives a protective layer—will keep them weatherproof. However, that's not something I tend to do because, for me, the rust spots are part of the attractive aesthetic. I do make sure, though, that I bring all my outdoor furniture under cover when the weather turns, to help prolong its life.

An alternative to wrought iron is cast-alloy furniture from the early twentieth century, which is robust and often very decorative. It also looks particularly good with a glossy paint finish, such as dark green or anthracite.

ABOVE This very rusty, old French café table and two slatted chairs, spattered with paint, will need a lot of work sanding and painting with a powder coating to restore them to how they once were. Provided they are completely safe to use, I would simply leave them as they are and enjoy their individuality.

OPPOSITE At the market in Montpellier in southwestern France, I spotted these metal garden chairs with their sold labels hanging from the scroll backs. The purchaser has undoubtedly bought them for their aged patina, just as I would have done.

ABOVE The antiques market at Isle-sur-la-Sorgue, in Provence, sees a number of vendors who have permanent stalls, which means they can be creative with their space. I love the arrangement of deer heads on the shutters here, but the main focus of the picture is the fern displayed on a very handsome brushed steel table. This would look wonderful in a yard full of greenery, but it would need a protective coating so that it could survive the elements.

RIGHT A set of rather unusual and charming, twisted metal chairs from the early nineteenth century—the rust certainly betrays their age and suggests that they have lived most of their life outdoors. In spite of their being a set, they are all slightly different because they are handmade, which adds to their appeal. The chair perched on the table is the child's chair in the group. A clear outdoor varnish will help preserve rusty chairs like these, and a cushion on the seat will help preserve you!

Reconstituted stone tables are lovely additions to the yard but they are not usually big enough to eat at. The best outdoor dining tables, seating more than six, are made of teak. Known for its durability and water resistance, teak has been used for centuries to build boats, and it's consequently a natural material for the garden. Applying teak oil will help prolong the life of the furniture, which could last 70 years or more. The color of the wood improves over the years, from its natural red/brown tone to a softer silver.

Fashion in the garden has, as for most things, changed over time. The late nineteenth century saw ornamental garden accessories, complemented by decorative metal furniture, usually painted white. Then, broadly speaking, in the twentieth century, the design of outdoor furniture was much the same as that indoors, with comfort and simplicity being of utmost importance. I am a great fan of the timeless designs of the American Walter Lamb. Ahead of his time with his passion for recycling, he used materials reclaimed from ships sunk during World War II. Pieces designed by him, however, are very hard to find now, and fetch a price much higher than I can afford.

You will always find matching chairs and tables. In particular abundance are French metal chairs with pretty curlicue backs and latticed or perforated seats. These designs hold their price and, if in good condition, a whole set will cost as much as buying new. However, I would never be tempted to buy a complete set because I prefer to have a mixture—of metal and wood, and some chairs with arms. A less contrived look feels more relaxing and inviting.

ABOVE Typical French metal scroll design garden tables like these will fetch a high price if they are in good condition. To restore them, paint with a powder coating or do nothing and enjoy the vintage look. The much more utilitarian orange tables on which they are displayed look like they have come from a café or restaurant. For similar pieces, ask the vendor for information on provenance, as well as advice on their care and likely durability.

OPPOSITE On my travels for this book, I came across a lot of reproduction garden furniture, like these metal chairs with their crisscross backs. Unfortunately, you will find both original and repro pieces at antique markets. The asking price is a good indicator of whether a piece is repro or not, as is its weight—original pieces will be heavier.

POTS AND ORNAMENTS

EARTHENWARE FLOWERPOTS, WHICH WERE FIRED ON BONFIRES OR IN FIRE PITS, ARE KNOWN TO HAVE EXISTED AS LONG AGO AS NEOLITHIC TIMES, AND THEY ARE STILL BEING DUG UP BY ARCHAEOLOGISTS ALL OVER THE WORLD. FROM THE BEGINNING, THEY WERE USED TO PROPAGATE PLANTS IN A CONTROLLED ENVIRONMENT, WHICH THEY STILL ARE.

The pots gained popularity simply as a means to transport plants from one place to another. In the eighteenth century, they became very fashionable and were an integral part of any well-kept yard. Josiah Wedgwood's flowerpots were even as famous as his dinnerware. Plant hunters and botanists used pots to ship seedlings, orchids, and violets from the West Indies, thereby beginning the spread of foreign plant species to Europe.

Typically, most garden pots are made from terra cotta. Caring for them couldn't be easier. Before planting them up or sowing seeds, mix a ratio of 1:10 bleach to water and submerge the pots in the water for about 30 minutes, or brush them with the solution if the pots are too large. Let them dry thoroughly before using. This is important to do so you don't risk transferring any diseases of previous plants to your new ones.

ABOVE Small terracotta pots, with their bases painted white, make very attractive table decorations with votive candles placed inside for summer parties. They can also be used for taller candles, held securely in soil or sand.

RIGHT A wall of used timber has been turned into a backdrop for this garden area at Big Daddy's Antiques, San Francisco. The three stone sinks or troughs would make great garden ornaments, while the stone ball, made from reconstituted stone (evident by the air holes), would be an intriguing talking point.

BELOW Another wonderful garden backdrop at Big Daddy's, this time of vintage apple crates, piled one on top of the other as display shelves for plants. The other elements are no less interesting: an old, circular, rough stone table and an ocher-glazed Anduze pot, with its typical garland design and potter's medal in the center.

Always clean the insides of your pots each time you plant them up. However, after the initial clean, I like to leave the outsides as they are. The elements will give your pots a character all of their own, perhaps adding moss or lichen. You can even encourage moss to form by coating the outside of the pot with yogurt.

Bear in mind that vintage terra-cotta pots will need bringing indoors before the frosts arrive, otherwise they are likely to crack.

Finding an Anduze pot is a great joy for me. Originally designed for the planting of lemon and orange trees, these famous stocky clay planters feature a garland of decorative plants on the outside and, if they are authentic, a stamp or badge showing the potter's name. The pots, as well as urns and jars, are still made today in Anduze, in the foothills of the Cévennes, in southern France. The colors you are most likely to come across in the markets are dark green and orange. If you are lucky, they can be hundreds of years old.

GARDEN ORNAMENTS

The garden ornaments on sale at flea markets take on so many guises. Birdbaths are perennial favorites—like many others, I love to sit quietly and watch the birds cleaning and preening themselves. Stone birdbaths are incredibly heavy and you may face transportation issues, but there are some lovely examples out there made of reconstituted stone, which are a lot lighter.

Old statues and sculptures, usually made of wood, stone, or marble, are a key design feature of many yards today. We have grown to love traditional figures, inspired by some of the more formal statues seen in the great

ABOVE A classical-style, cast-iron plant urn. Pieces like this are easily spruced up, with a wire brush, to remove all the loose rust, and then with sandpaper, followed by spraying with an outdoor primer and painting. Alternatively, you could simply leave well alone and enjoy them as they are.

BELOW RIGHT One or more of these Turkish oil or wine flagons could be up to 150 years old. Appreciated for their beautiful patina, these containers would look good grouped together in a yard or brought indoors as a decorative touch to a kitchen.

gardens of Europe. Classical figures are very popular, as are stone lions, often seen at the entrance to a house, symbolizing protection.

Trickling water is both soothing to the ear and the eye. For that reason, fountains have become very popular in yards, but remember that you will you need to employ a gardening contractor, or even a plumber, to reconnect the fountain with a water supply.

Vintage pots and urns, many from Turkey and Morocco, have become important decorative additions to the garden. Once used for oil or wine, these containers are never bought for their original purpose at the markets, where they feature regularly. Often with a wonderful patina, they make lovely containers for specimen plants or simply left empty. Their use, though, isn't restricted to the yard—they look great displayed in the home as well. Similarly, items intended originally for the home could be given a new lease of life in the yard, such as mirrors, to create extra light and cast reflections, or sieves, to act as plant containers.

ABOVE On sale at the antiques market in Isle-sur-la-Sorgue, Provence, these decorative vintage iron railings would make a striking backdrop in a yard, propped up against a fence. As with all antique metal, sanding and repainting them would give protection from further wear. Climbing plants could even be encouraged to grow up them. Of course, the railings could always be repaired by a blacksmith and used once more as they were originally intended.

ABOVE The word "Garden" has been spelt out in three-dimensional letters for a fun piece of outdoor decoration. The letters are new but made to look old and rusty.

LEFT An old, shell-shaped garden planter, filled with plants and featuring a metal cow in the middle. Such original and quirky ways of displaying items for sale are all part of what makes shopping at flea markets so much fun.

ABOVE A huge pair of corrugated doors in this vast hangar at Round Top Antiques Fair, Texas, is the backdrop to two cast-iron urns. With rust showing through the white paint, the urns are showing the markings of time, which makes them particularly attractive to a buyer after the shabby, distressed look. The pair of wooden finials, perched on top of the gates, would make very attractive indoor ornaments, table centers, or mantel displays.

LEFT Keep an eye open for anything that could be turned into an unusual plant container. This vintage grape harvest basket made of wicker could conceal a plastic pot with a plant or be lined with plastic and then planted up using potting compost. It could also make a delightful sconce, with the candles secured into position with soil or sand.

GARDEN EQUIPMENT

TOOLS ARE A POPULAR MAINSTAY OF FLEA MARKETS. OLD PARAPHERNALIA IS ALWAYS INTRIGUING, AS IT CAN HAVE SO MANY USES APART FROM ITS ORIGINAL PURPOSE. I LOVE THE IDEA OF USING BIG DUTCH WATERING CANS, OLD WASHING DOLLIES, AND WHEELBARROWS AS PLANTERS, OR HORSE TROUGHS AS BIRDBATHS. THE LIST IS ENDLESS AND YOUR SEARCH WILL BE A REWARDING JOURNEY OF DISCOVERY.

ABOVE You will undoubtedly come across a number of items for sale that you consider are just not worth paying good money for, like this very battered watering can, which doesn't look like it could be repaired or made useful in another role. However, some people might think otherwise…

Buying tools or old garden equipment can be very satisfying. For the keen gardener, the better the quality of tools, the easier it is to perform the necessary chores, and old garden tools are often better made by artisans skilled at wood- and metalwork. With a little effort from you, their creations can be brought back to life. As with all wooden items, garden tools, from fork and trowel handles to wooden wheelbarrows, should be checked for woodworm. If woodworm is still present, the holes will look freshly made and there are likely to be traces of sawdust. You could give affected pieces a wide berth or take your chances and treat with a good-quality woodworm treatment when you get home. Handles can be sanded, waxed, and polished, while metal can be sanded down to remove any rust, then oiled. Vintage garden implements have already stood the test of time and will continue to do so with a little TLC.

Older and larger garden implements and farm implements, often from the nineteenth century, can make great features for the yard. Many of those found at flea markets, such as buckets, cans, washing dollies, and milk churns, will be galvanized, making them ideal garden planters (galvanization is the process of applying a protective zinc coating to steel or iron, making it water- and weatherproof). Before the invention of the washing machine, the galvanized washing dolly, or ribbed bucket, was used, along with a long wooden contraption, resembling a milking stool on a stick, that agitated the washing while it was in the tub. These dolly tubs make incredibly attractive planters for a small tree or a shrub, but you will need to drill some holes in the bottom before planting up.

ABOVE Just a few holes drilled into the bottom of these galvanized milk pails for drainage will turn them into efficient plant containers. Although they are handsome enough as they are, they would also look very smart if whitewashed, especially when planted with spring-flowering bulbs.

Cleaning galvanized objects is easy, but don't use any abrasive products or hard bristles because the metal is quite soft. As always, the beauty of the item is in the aging—if, for example, you want a shiny bucket, it would be much cheaper to buy a new one from the hardware store. Like the dolly tub, a bucket will need some holes drilled in the bottom to allow for drainage, if you intend to use it as a planter.

Far too heavy and difficult to maneuver, old wooden wheelbarrows are not very efficient in their dedicated role. However, when planted up, they make very attractive decorative features, as do old ladders, propped up against the wall with pots fixed to each rung, milking stools, and horse troughs, with or without plants.

Vintage stone in the yard, covered in moss, is very desirable and it can come in many forms. You may be lucky enough to find a tether stone. This big, heavy lump of stone with a giant hook embedded into it was used in the early nineteenth century for tethering a horse. Now these vestiges of a bygone age can be used as doorstops or purely decoratively.

ABOVE LEFT A wonderful group of tether stones, with their big rusty metal hooks or rings, once used for tethering horses, would make a lovely historic feature in a yard. The reconstituted stone spheres, covered in moss and grouped together in the stone bowl, would also make a unique, ground-level attraction.

ABOVE A field full of milk pails, no longer fit for purpose, interspersed with the odd watering can. Although the pails have aesthetic appeal, I can think of very little practical use for them, except, perhaps, removing the lids and filling them with dried flowers, such as hydrangeas, or shapely twigs like contorted hazel. I can, though, see them lined up neatly against an old garden wall just being themselves.

LEFT A little imagination can create brand new roles for all sorts of objects. These grain storage tins were used originally to keep chicken feed dry during the nineteenth century, but their cylindrical shapes and wide necks mean they are also well suited to becoming flower or plant pots.

ABOVE A clever wall display of wooden boxes, weathered and aged to an attractive silver, with a potted plant in each cubby hole. Seen here at Big Daddy's Antiques in San Francisco, such a wall would be easy to replicate in your own outside space, with the boxes screwed onto a fence.

BOXES AND CRATES

Up until the mid-1950s, all fruit and vegetables would have been displayed for sale in their original wooden shipping crates, and most of these would have featured a label—often very pretty and colorful—depicting the farm or orchard where the produce originated. The slatted wood sides and base kept the air circulating and the produce fresh, ready for market. Sadly, the practice ended when cardboard boxes were introduced for the purpose. Potato chitting trays, used for sprouting potatoes, are similar to fruit crates but with lower sides.

There are vintage wooden crates, boxes, and trays aplenty in flea markets today. They can be used for many purposes but more so inside the house. They make authentic and original containers in just about any room, but look especially good and rustic on kitchen shelves, holding an array of cooking essentials. Chitting trays, meanwhile, are just the right size to act as filing trays in a home office—and they are so much better looking than plastic trays.

Outdoors, these containers make gorgeous shelving units for plants, massed together and fixed to a wall or fence, as in the picture on the left. If you do decide to use them outdoors, you can extend their life by coating them in a clear, matte varnish.

RIGHT A Japanese acer is a beautiful frothy companion for this old molded stone planter. The missing foot is no reason not to buy it—for the right price. To make it stable, you can easily prop it up with a wedge of wood. Displayed on their ends, the vintage fruit crates seem to be calling out to be filled with books for the home or with tiny pots of cacti for the yard.

DIRECTORY

THE REAL JOY FOR ME OF SHOPPING AT FLEA MARKETS IS FINDING THE UNEXPECTED. I HAVE MANY TREASURES IN MY HOME THAT I SIMPLY FELL UPON BY CHANCE. THESE PIECES ARE INCREDIBLY IMPORTANT TO ME, PARTLY BECAUSE THEY ARE IRREPLACEABLE BUT QUITE OFTEN BECAUSE OF THEIR AGING AND PATINA. ALL SORTS OF THINGS, FROM BUSTS AND TRAYS TO POTS AND TRINKET BOWLS, HAVE FOUND A HOME IN MY APARTMENT, AND I WILL NEVER PART WITH THEM.

They are memories of a time, a country, an event, and they all work together to make my home different from everyone else's. This is the reason why, whenever I find myself with time to spare in a new city, I always try to seek out the local markets.

The following list of flea markets around the world includes my favorites plus many which have been recommended to me by friends and other flea-market aficionados. The dates of markets can vary, so always check their websites for dates and opening times before you visit. Tourist and town information centers will also be able to provide details of local markets, as will the listings sections of local newspapers.

Visiting flea markets can sometimes be a little hit-and-miss. Occasionally you will visit and not find anything to your liking, but more often than not, the hardest thing is limiting the number of items you buy.

UNITED STATES

ALAMEDA POINT ANTIQUES FAIRE
2700 Saratoga Street
Alameda
CA 94501
Held on the first Sunday of every month,
10am to 5pm
www.alamedapointantiquesfaire.com

ROUND TOP ANTIQUES FAIR
Round Top
Texas
Held in spring and fall.
www.roundtoptexasantiques.com
Visit the website for on-site shippers

BRIMFIELD
Brimfield
Massachusetts
Held three times a year: May, July,
September
www.brimfieldshows.com
Visit the website for on-site shippers

BROOKLYN FLEA

Held at three New York locations:
Brooklyn, Fort Greene, Williamsburg
Opening times vary so check the
 website.
www.brooklynflea.com

CHELSEA ANTIQUES GARAGE

West 25th St
New York
Every Saturday and Sunday. Also runs
a market in Hell's Kitchen.
www.annexmarkets.com

GEORGETOWN FLEA MARKET

Wisconsin Ave, north of S St
Washington DC
Held every Sunday
www.georgetownfleamarket.com

ROSEBOWL ANTIQUES MARKET

Pasadena
Los Angeles
CA 91103
Held on the second Sunday of every
month; admission times and prices vary.
Other markets linked to this one include:

VENTURA FLEA MARKET
SAN BERNARDINO OUTDOOR MARKET
BEAUMONT OUTDOOR MARKET
BEAUMONT GARAGE SALE

Detailed info on each market available
at the website below:
www.rgcshows.com

MELROSE TRADING POST

Los Angeles
CA
See website for locations and times
www.melrosetradingpost.org

BIG DADDY'S

3334 La Cienega Place
Los Angeles
CA 90016
Open 7 days a week. Check website
for times.

Also at:
1550 17th Street
San Francisco
CA 94107
Open Monday to Saturday. Check
website for times.
www.bdantiques.com